W9-CQT-148

ANGELIC MESSENGER

C·A·R·D·S

ANGELIC MESSENGER
C · A · R · D · S

A Divination System for Spiritual Discovery

MEREDITH L. YOUNG-SOWERS

Photography by Carol Duke

STILLPOINT

STILLPOINT PUBLISHING
Building a society that honors The Earth,
Humanity, and The Sacred in All Life.

For a free catalog or ordering information, write
Stillpoint Publishing, Box 640, Walpole, NH 03608, USA
or call
1-800-847-4014 TOLL FREE (Continental US, except NH)
1-603-756-9281 (Foreign and NH)

This book is manufactured in the United States of America.
Cover and text design by Karen Savary

Published by Stillpoint Publishing, Box 640,
Meetinghouse Road, Walpole, NH 03608

ISBN 0-913299-95-2

Library of Congress Catalog Card Number: 93-85594

3 5 7 9 8 6 4

This book is printed on acid-free recycled paper
to save trees and preserve Earth's ecology.

Dedication

To the angels, those harbingers of a world to come, a world that holds the compassion and love that we long for;

To the beings of light who hold us when we are despondent and afraid and who lead us into the light when we are unable to see;

To the master teachers and guardians of our lives and our planet, whose unfailing wisdom and grace enlighten and empower all living things:

Especially to Mentor, my own master teacher, whose guidance has taught me of a world that could be and would be now and ever more;

To all of the nonphysical world that is available to our inquisitive ear and trained eye, we offer our appreciation for these opportunities to experience God.

Contents

Acknowledgments

These cards are the result of the accumulated effort of many wonderful people who have given freely of their wisdom, their advice, and their skill. I specifically want to thank:

- my best friend and dear husband, Errol, for his skill as my editor, his willingness to take on additional business and household tasks to free up my time to write, for the weekends spent in the office encouraging my efforts to draw from the wisdom of the angels, and for his lasting and unwavering love and support.

- my friend Carol Duke, who came into my life as if drawn by the Universe at just the right time, and whose magnificent photographs of the flower images in these cards inspired my writing.

- Stillpoint's art director and designer, Karen Savary, whose unfailing patience and creative brilliance as both an artist and a designer is so evident in the artwork that graces these beautiful cards, the guidebook, and the display case.

- my friend and assistant, Gisela Rank, who originally found photographer Carol Duke and whose continued good cheer and deep belief in the angelic realm has encouraged me through the many months of the project's writing and development.

- Stillpoint's senior editor, Dorothy Seymour, whose skillful copyediting of the book helped me write with greater clarity and whose willingness to work weekends and late nights enabled me to meet my writing deadline.

- Stillpoint's typesetter, Sally Nichols, for her keen attention and care in bringing the text of this book to life.

- Stillpoint staff members Virginia Page, Karin Bell, Philip Conover, Lynn Malaguti, and Joe Murphy, for picking up the slack and supporting me during the time I was creating this project.

- our friends Barbara and Jerry Clow, the owners of Bear & Company and originators of *The Medicine Cards*, for their encouragement and support.

- Ralph Blum, author of *The Book of Runes*, and his wife Jeanne, for their friendship and deep desire to experience the truth of this life's spiritual journey.

Preface

In this moment, the angels are talking with you through their messengers, the flowers. Profoundly beautiful, entirely different and unique, each flower has its own reflection of the heavenly teachers that seek to guide you in love.

Flowers have a physical presence that we are the most familiar with because they grace our gardens, homes, and celebrations. Flowers also have an emotional presence that is complementary to our own. Flower essences, for example, have for years been used by many people to help restore their inner balance and emotional harmony. But flowers also have a spiritual quality that has never been fully explored before, perhaps because we've not been ready to understand that all living things share a common bond of life force that is decidedly spiritual, and because the need has never been quite so pressing for people to learn from their personal guidance.

It has become clear to me over many years of working with flowers in my own garden that there is a transcendent quality to flowers that helps us touch our own inner joy and exquisite nature as part of God. Flowers are the angelic messengers in our lives, helping us understand that we have something unique to contribute to life even if we're not yet sure exactly what that is. The angels guide us through their flower messengers to become more sensitive and accepting of the innate creativity and profound wisdom that we hold within us. And they encourage us to honor and protect the wide diversity of life forms so that we will have a more meaningful sustainable planetary home.

Deciding to work with these cards heralds the beginning of a powerful new chapter in your life. Whether you are a seasoned spiritual traveler or not, the angels will help you in ways most appropriate to your search. The angels will encourage and support your changes, hold you when you hurt, accept you when no one else does, and offer you the wisdom to step out of guilt and self-recrimination. The angels will teach you to value yourself as an essential aspect of the Divine. As you use these Angelic Messenger Cards you will find a profound sense of joy that emerges into all arenas of your life.

Angels guide our lives even if we do not see or hear them. Yet perhaps we are now ready to know what they would have us believe and understand. Through these cards you will come to experience the guidance and love that you may find nowhere else in your life. And by using these cards on a daily basis, you can expand your perceptual abilities to interpret the guidance meant just for you.

And so the importance of this single moment lies in your ability to spread your wings and to breathe in the goodness of life and the beauty all around you. It is also to keep your eyes open to really seeing the people, animals, and living systems that are suffering in the world. How can you help change the world? Is it the grandest delusion of all to think that you can make a difference? Is it narcissistic to be concerned with your own meditations and personal spiritual journey when the world is in such trauma?

My feeling is that the only way we can make things better in the world is to first address them at the personal level in our own lives. We can, and will, live only what we truly believe and value. We hold in our hearts the ability to provide for all living things. When this realization becomes our mandate for living, then we know that the spirit of love is burning brightly in our hearts and our lives.

As you work with these cards and the guidance of the angels you will find that you feel love more intensely for all things. You may feel this love, for example, in a walk that might take you into the forest of tall, majestic pine trees, in the silence of your meditations, in the songs of the birds in your garden, or in time spent with your children or other people. These things will touch you in new ways because your spirit has ignited your full range of emotional participation.

As you increasingly treasure the beauty in the flowers and Nature, you will also rediscover the buried treasure of your divine essence, your own soul.

Meredith L. Young-Sowers
Walpole, New Hampshire
July 21, 1993

Introduction to the Angelic Realm

Have you ever wondered if there really are angels? Most of us have an image of angels as gently loving beings that somehow hover around us even though we are unable to see them. Angels fulfill this image of enlightened beings, but they are a great deal more, and they are very, very real.

Angels, rather than being merely a metaphor for the company of heaven, are actual energy beings, or beings of light that are ever-present in our lives. They seek to remind us of our spiritual heritage and to act as teachers, masters, and avatars. Whether we believe in Jesus Christ, Buddha, Mohammed, or Krishna as the enlightened teacher we most admire and feel drawn to, we are also blessed with the presence of the angels. These beings of light have much to share with us to help us understand the nature of our existence and the ways to create loving and successful lives.

Angels are teachers who are drawn into people's lives much as any spiritual teacher and student become connected: through what may seem to be synchronicity—being in the right place at the right time—and through a willingness and desire to learn of spiritual things. My feeling is that angels are always present to us. I also feel it is our deepest innate intention to understand the loving quality of our own spirits that allows us to form bonds with these beings.

MENTOR: MY INSPIRATION FOR THE
ANGELIC MESSENGER CARDS

For well over a decade, I've been taught by an angelic presence that describes himself/herself simply as Mentor, meaning "teacher." Before it was generally accepted that we each had access to meaningful divine guidance, I found myself drawn into a mystical experience that foretold of my own unfolding spiritual work and the reality of the nonphysical angelic world. I was shown that direct guidance would increasingly become available to every person who sought it, and that our guides and teachers would be forthcoming in their wisdom to help us through the planetary complexities that lay before us. I had no spiritual ax to grind, no desire to even experience the angelic realm, yet I found and forged this bond apparently through my deep desire to understand the nature of pain in people's lives and how I might help alleviate it. For years I accepted Mentor's teachings only on the surface level as beautiful words, because in my heart I didn't truly believe that angels were real.

I've written the story of my meeting this extraordinary teacher and the nature of his/her presence in my first book, *Agartha, A Journey to the Stars.* Now, many years after the initial meeting and through my struggle to find and value Mentor's enlightened teachings, I have found that when we cease to struggle with our spiritual nature and allow its simple beauty and peace to arise from within us, we see the face of the Divine most accurately.

After years of knowing Mentor's gentle but assured teachings as to the nature of life, death, and awareness, I no longer have reason to question his/her motives or means of reaching me. I accept both the wisdom I receive and the process of receiving it, for the deep all-encompassing love that is conveyed is evidence to me of its truth.

Each person perceives the spiritual dimensions of life differently, and each finds his or her own most appropriate and meaningful path to the light. It has always been true that the significance of our guidance lies not in the process of receiving it but in the lasting quality of the insight received and its ability to lift us into awareness and over our most difficult human hurdles. No two people are the same, and no two spiritual interactions are the same, either. We can be moved most profoundly by our angelic teachers working through us to help us awaken our own inner awareness and through this experience to lay the groundwork for a more meaningful life.

As we step along our spiritual path with the angels, we will never again be so confounded that we lose our faith or be so discouraged, distressed, or filled with fear that we are unable to go on, whether that means staying on the Earth or leaving it. Our journey is to seek and to accept the blessings of life and the learning implicit in those blessings for future personal and planetary well-being. The angels are available; it is we humans who are learning to listen.

SEARCHING FOR OUR SPIRITUAL ROOTS THAT ARE THE BASIS FOR ENLIGHTENMENT

Many of us in Western culture are searching for the perfect blend of our spiritual heritage. We may have grown up as Christians or Jews, but many of us left behind a structure that seemed cumbersome and seemed lacking in meaning and relevance for our lives and our struggles. We want, and are finding, a more expansive and universal doctrine of spiritual truth, and it is coming to us as our own unique blend of spiritual teaching that we compile ourselves from many enlightened sources.

Beneath the swings of our moods and the incessant pangs of happiness and despair lies the world of our spirit, our inner mind. We search for serenity and self-realization because we recognize that this spiritual quest is the journey of our life. And we are drawn into the world of spirit and those who mysteriously open the gates of our awareness because we want to understand and live the purpose for which we incarnated.

Every day we create, formulate, and translate inspiration and wisdom into our own sacred writings. In doing so, each of us discovers that truth is truth, that one person's truth may be stated differently from another's, but it is the same insight and inspiration that formed the original mystical basis for the world's religions. Sacred writings are the materials written down to preserve the teachings of a master teacher. For many of us the angels are the master teachers, and it is into their realm that we seek to move when using these *Angelic Messenger Cards* to glean insight and wisdom.

Time is the ultimate spiritual tool, because if we stay long enough with a regimen of daily spiritual study, we gradually find the inner states of balance and love that we come to accept as our spirit. I realize that the kind of love we are taught by our angelic teachers is not initially of our comprehension. Yet in searching for the means of healing ourselves and our planet, it is from this source of enlightenment that we can learn to love with our spirits rather than only with our emotions.

FINDING AND FORGING BONDS WITH OUR OWN ANGELIC TEACHERS

Even if we lack belief in them, we have angelic teachers. When we no longer need to prove that we can survive without help, we are ready to take advantage of the opportunities for angelic guidance. Life is meant to be more than mere survival. I believe we are meant to prosper and to learn the means of discovering cooperative, peaceful, and joyful ways of living together and learning from each other. Do we know how to do this at the moment? No, but we are learning by quantum leaps. Our angelic teachers are helping us.

Making room for the impressions of our angelic teachers is similar to the fractional pause we take naturally between breaths. We experience inner spaces when we are able to hesitate between our daily thoughts and inner chatter. When a space is available between individual mental thoughts, then we are able to slowly widen these mental openings so that a very different kind of energy pattern is observable.

This spiritual energy pattern is free-flowing and contours easily around any suggestion or question. As you go about your daily living in an open and responsive mode, you might ask yourself, for instance, "What meaning does my life have?" Your angelic teachers might answer your question in the following way in a sequential unfolding of events and insights. Your eyes might fall casually upon a nearby tree. Suddenly a bird lands on the top branch. From within your inner free space comes the realization that you are like this bird and that your life brings something totally unique and vital to life in general, which is represented by the tree. You may feel an inspiration to bring into the world your own hidden abilities and creativity because you sense the profound significance of each living thing bringing its greatest gift to the tree of life. What a realization!

In addition to using free association, we can also enhance the quality and meaning coming into our lives daily from our angelic teachers by placing in our hearts "a standing order" for guidance of any kind. We might repeat to ourselves, "I ask that my heart's truest intention be always heard and known by the Universe, and that all my angelic teachers understand my desire to learn spiritually whenever possible."

Working with your inner spiritual spaces is a marvelous way to expand your creative vision. Accessing your spiritual spaces is the means through which you will be able to effectively learn from the flowers that are the angels' messengers. The greater your natural creativity, imagination, and ability to draw meaning from images or archetypal patterns and symbology, the more fun and meaning you will derive from working with the *Angelic Messenger Cards*.

THE ANGELS SPEAK TO US THROUGH FLOWERS

We see the beauty of flowers each day and yet rarely take the time to look deeply into their presence. They are the faces of our angelic teachers, metaphorically, and perhaps actually, since angels are energy, pure vibrations of light, and they can be manifested in any way that brings beauty and inspiration. These Angelic Messenger Cards take you within the flower and within yourself to study your extraordinary human nature as you study the nature of the flower.

Guidance happens through a reverent observation of the flowers. The angelic messengers, the flowers, carry the greatest and most profound messages from the angels that humanity is ever likely to hear—and they are available to all of us all the time.

Today more than ever we find ourselves ready to open our hearts to the angels and archangels that we've always loved and honored from a distance. Talking to angels is the natural extension of the channeling phenomenon of the late 1970s and '80s, when we realized that the levels of non-physical life were an available and abundant resource for direct relationship with all levels of Divinity. No wonder we plunged into channeling with such exuberance!

The Buddhists speak of channeling as the merger of the wisdom mind of the Buddha with the *rigpa*, or inner mind of the student. As many of us sought to really know God for the first time, we experienced the brilliance of direct guidance that so shifted and transformed our lives that our hearts were opened to the master teachers and angelic beings. We accepted that we had a future on the Earth, and that the Earth was our mother, our home, and we were responsible for her very existence.

In recent years we've grown more introspective, more able to perceive and extend our perceptual abilities into clairvoyance and clairaudience. We've learned to read the physical, emotional, and spiritual energies of other people as well as of animals and plants. We've learned that a holistic approach to all healing is essential. We've learned that miracles are everyday occurrences. We've delighted in feeling God's breath as the wind in the trees and God's grace reflected in the incomparable intricacies of Nature's beauty.

Flowers and the angels that speak through them are the connecting links that hold our physical lives in perfect relationship to the heavenly realms.

FLOWERS HAVE A SPIRITUAL LIFE, TOO

When I first started to work with the beings and energy sources that are abundant in every organic garden, I realized that flowers have a spiritual life path. Flowers seek more than the physical sun; they seek identification with all manner of spiritual energy to encourage their own spiritual growth.

From Mentor I learned that humanity was walking a tightrope with the natural world. In years past the plants, trees, and flowers had trusted us human beings to be their companions on this spiritual journey. But in the last four or five decades we have let our companions down by cutting, plundering, and ripping at the Earth in so many ways that Nature is beginning to withdraw her invitation to us. It is unthinkable to me that we would some day in the not-too-distant future walk our path in isolation. Perhaps we're seeing the beginning of this separation from Nature in the growing maelstrom of physical disasters.

Yet the angelic messengers, the flowers that fill the still-remaining open spaces, pepper the fields with their wild and carefree presences, reign regally over our formal gardens, and joyfully climb the arbors and arches overlooking our country garden beds, tell us that we still have time to reverse the damage and to open our hearts to a genuinely spiritual quality of life that offers a reverence for all things.

Inadvertently seeking a pardon from Nature, we've sought flowers as medicine to heal our bodies. We've used flower essences to help us heal our emotional traumas and to find solace and inner strength. But flowers also have a spiritual aspect that offers us the profound spiritual reflection of the angels who oversee their existence and our own. And it is this ability of flowers to reflect angelic guidance that is the power of the *Angelic Messenger Cards*.

A Divination System for Receiving Angelic Guidance

Angelic Messenger Cards offer spiritual seekers a unique and effective tool for developing a direct and meaningful relationship with the Divine through the messages of angelic teachers. The cards act as a "living prayer" to help us resolve problems, develop inner trust, affirm ourselves, and renew and awaken the spiritual energy of love.

Used as a tool for self-reflection, the cards and the accompanying guidebook help us accept daily struggles as spiritual challenges. Using one of several card spreads or layouts and referring to this guidebook for accompanying teachings, we are better able to pinpoint the specific spiritual challenges we face, gain new awareness of ways to meet those challenges through the "angelic messages," and discover the spiritual opportunities available to us and the practical means of applying our new insights.

THE BLUEPRINT FOR LIVING SPIRITUALLY THAT UNDERLIES THE ANGELIC MESSENGER CARDS

In my book, *Spiritual Crisis: What's Really Behind Loss, Disease, and Life's Major Hurts* (Stillpoint Publishing, 1993), I explain in great detail the six aspects of the energy of love (spiritual energy) that influence our lives continuously. These influences are: Reflection, Partnership, Integration, Alignment, Rejuvenation, and Nourishment. I have set up the *Angelic Messenger Cards* in the same way.

In *Spiritual Crisis* I note that: "In order to understand our spiritual energy in these six major aspects we need to develop skills of intuition and deeper awareness through meditation or quiet periods of reflection that can educate us adequately to our own level of truth and to the influences of love. We experience the energy of love in our lives in many different ways, and each has something important to tell us about ourselves and our inner health." The *Angelic Messenger Cards* are uniquely designed to help us experience this energy of love.

Because the *Angelic Messenger Cards* are a divinely-inspired tool for spiritual self-discovery and have their foundation in truly understanding and using love as a universal energy, they carry the seeds of both personal and planetary transformation. This transformation requires us to accept love in the larger perspective—namely, that love is the opportunity to grow into our own greatest potential while maintaining the balance of the whole. This definition of love implies that we are responsible to ourselves to grow spiritually. At the same time we are responsible to support the growth of other living things in order to perpetuate the whole system. The energy of love involves more than absorbing energy; it also requires our giving back so that ultimately the health of the entire system feeds back through us and all other living things to give love and life.

As we approach the next millennium, we are being called to live with greater awareness of our own spiritual natures as well as our interrelationships with God and all other living things. It is therefore essential that we consider the spiritual influences that all living things are touched by and that we as people are being called to acknowledge.

The six spiritual energy influences of love give us the inner impulse that calls us to live in those ways that are most supportive of our individual spiritual growth and a balanced relationship with all other life. Any level of lasting healing requires our conscious use of these spiritual energy influences in order to live a balanced, healthy life in harmony with God.

UNDERSTANDING HOW THE ANGELIC MESSENGER CARDS CAN ADVANCE YOUR SPIRITUAL INSIGHT AND CREATE A BALANCED LIFE

In the set of *Angelic Messenger Cards* are seven cards that relate to each one of the six aspects of spiritual energy, love. These forty-two cards plus six wild cards comprise the complete set. Together, the six aspects of spiritual energy form a circle, reflecting the continuous cycles of life and death, awareness and confrontation, movement from spirit to ego and back to spirit.

THE SIX ASPECTS OF SPIRITUAL ENERGY

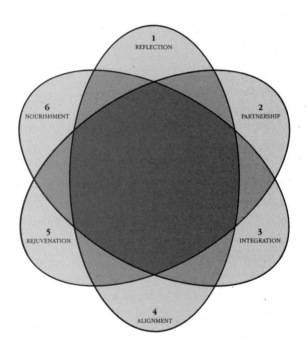

Imagine that, all together, these forty-eight cards form a giant wheel, with each card playing a part in helping you gain inner wisdom to heal physically and emotionally and, what is even more significant, to find and advance your spiritual insight into the nature of your life. This is no small order, but we are on the Earth to learn.

We might think of these six aspects of love as forming a plan or model for spiritual liberation. When we are able to free ourselves from the cycles of our external world, even to loosen the hold our physical and emotional realities have over our true spiritual clarity, then we are free to experience spirit and to learn more directly from the angelic realms.

As described in my book, *Spiritual Crisis*, these six aspects of spiritual energy are the basis for a balanced life and are the essential elements of our inner life. They maintain and recreate our health day by day. As we change and grow spiritually through our life, we become more aware of the causes of our discontent, and conversely we grow in our ability to glean from the angelic realms.

A more expanded definition for each of the six aspects of love, spiritual energy, would be:

1. *Reflection:* Becoming aware of your divine self
2. *Partnership:* Growing spiritually in relationships
3. *Integration:* Establishing an inner harmony among the body, mind, and spirit
4. *Alignment:* Performing meaningful work that grows from your divinely-inspired life purpose
5. *Rejuvenation:* Participating with nature in the cycles of life for your personal renewal
6. *Nourishment:* Choosing thoughts, foods, and emotional responses that give you spiritual fulfillment

THE SIX ASPECTS OF SPIRITUAL ENERGY AND
THEIR CARD GROUPS

As you work with the *Angelic Messenger Cards*, it is essential that you deepen your understanding of the spiritual truth and awareness specific to each aspect of spiritual energy and its corresponding group of seven cards.

Cards of Reflection (Numbers 1–7, purple)

The cards of *Reflection* help you build an ever-deepening relationship with God. These cards cause you to question the core beliefs that you hold about your life and about your relationship with the divine Source. These cards are the foundation cards for this set and speak to the spiritual beliefs that you've accumulated over your lifetime. By drawing one or more of these cards, you are being called to transcend apparent loss, failure, or stagnation by accepting that you are undergoing a deeply significant spiritual transformation. When you pull one of these cards, you are being asked to focus on the possibilities for your life through a return to basic beliefs to rediscover a quality of divine love that will help you benefit from your efforts and choices. You are being guided to open your heart to the sacred in all life.

Cards of Partnership (Numbers 8–14, red)

The cards of *Partnership* awaken you to a different potential for all of your relationships. These cards are encouraging you to seek better communications in your relationships and to personally accept responsibility for creating meaningful interactions with others based on your own ability to love and forgive without judgement. When you draw one or more of these cards, you are being guided to see that your relationships are a reflection of your beliefs about God and about yourself.

Relationships allow you to work through your own limiting control and power issues while invoking a deeper presence of divine love to bring you and others into harmony. These cards prepare you to understand and create on the planet a partnership way of living, whether it be with children, a partner, close friends, or those people you work with. In drawing these cards, you are being supported in the changes you intuitively feel you need to make in your relationships. You are being guided in seeking more meaningful and lasting relationships based on shared spiritual values.

Cards of Integration (Numbers 15–21, orange)

The cards of Integration alert you to a need for inner balance and a life that more fully supports your own spiritually-guided beliefs. These cards carry the energy of holistic healing by helping you identify those long-standing mental messages that you have been sending to your body that reflect emotional need rather than spiritual support and self-love. You are encouraged, through these cards, to accept the healer within you and to realize that your body, mind, and spirit make up one integrated energy system. You draw one or more of these cards when you are in need of more confidence in your ability to act according to your real feelings and when you seek to break down old barriers that have walled off your spirit and/or your feelings from your physical body and your physical needs.

Through integrating your spirit's love with your body and emotions, you bring about self-healing and life healing. These cards also speak to the ways in which your efforts serve to encourage planetary healing through holistic means.

Cards of Alignment (Numbers 22–28, yellow)

The cards of Alignment focus your attention on your means of service, the life work you've chosen or desire to discover. These cards are meant to help you understand the true nature of your life's service by showing you that you are already living it in some form. When you draw one or more of these cards, you are learning to pull strength from your daily spiritual practices in order to bring your vision and its physical man-

ifestation into greater clarity. You are also helped to appreciate that in accepting your own worth and paying attention to
your own natural patterns of working, living, and sharing, you
see the form your life work is taking. In drawing these cards,
you confront your ego's needs to have your work attain importance or become highly visible. You are able to identify the
patterns of expectation and approval that may stand in the
way of your accepting the simplicity and true meaning of your
service. These cards offer you a means of valuing your own
capacity for love, kindness, and compassion in order to benefit from the joy of living in alignment with your purpose.

Cards of Rejuvenation (Numbers 29–35, green)

The cards of *Rejuvenation* are meant to help you see Nature's
processes as teachers for your own essential changes. While
Nature is often held up as humankind's teacher, these cards
offer you a more immediate means of using Nature in learning
to value your own life and to live in the moment. Nature
teaches you of the inevitability of change and encourages you
to enjoy the shifts between the focused attention of intense
emotional involvement and the pure rejuvenation of relaxation. In drawing one or more of these cards, you are accepting that you can set aside your stress and accept life on its
own terms without struggle, absorbing the beauty and fullness
that Nature offers you. When you draw a *Rejuvenation* card,
you are being guided to take more time for yourself as a means
of reaffirming your joy in living and your belief in your ability
to live purposefully and gently on the Earth. You are being
directed to look outside and inside your own life to find a
more relaxed means of self-expression and to accept the freedom to live each moment as if it were your last.

Cards of Nourishment (Numbers 36–42, blue)

The cards of *Nourishment* speak to the ways you can feel more
supported by your life. Choice is the significant theme in
these cards. You are guided to evaluate the daily flow of your

life and the decisions or lack of decisions that determine the overall quality and meaning you derive from living. You are asked to stop and listen to your spirit before choosing self-defeating and disempowering ways of accepting life at the lowest level. These cards guide you to accept a different belief about your future and your ability to bring love into your life from your spirit and in order to attract to yourself the support that you need.

When you draw one or more of these cards of *Nourishment*, you are being shown the means to find nourishment from within yourself, nourishment that can balance your needs with those of the planet. You are also shown how to discover an inner meaning to your life so that you can move toward spiritual self-sufficiency and the creation of a meaningful life-style. These cards guide you to seek a different means of being nourished by your life and a readiness to identify the subtle factors or hidden addictions and agendas that drain your creativity and your belief in yourself.

Wild Cards of Divine Guidance

These four wild cards have particular power to help you perceive a spiritual encounter that is ready to emerge into your life. You are being guided to accept that, in certain ways, you will be able to more easily put your fears and uneasiness to rest, because you are being shown the reality of the nonphysical world, of God, and/or of the spirit of someone you've loved and who has died. Drawing one of these wild cards of *Divine Guidance* is a direct response to your prayers, meditations, or invocations in which you have been seeking to know or experience God more directly, to find or hear your teachers more specifically, or to interact with the nonphysical world of angels in a more direct way. You have drawn a *Divine Guidance* card to alert you to a situation, event, or breakthrough opportunity that you might otherwise have missed. Your own intuition guides you to know when the Universe is especially close to you, informing you that you will be able to glean a specific message that in some way is very important for you to know. These are cards of miracles and awakening, of hope and joy, manifested in response to your prayers.

Wild Cards of Abundance

These two cards offer you a different view of abundant living by alerting you to impending opportunities for abundance and a means of evaluating your decisions according to spiritual criteria rather than only ego-centered ones. These opportunities may have to do with financial resources becoming available to you, or a positive turn of events in a relationship. The opportunities now available to you portend a positive increase in the specific means of abundance that you have been seeking. *Abundance* cards ask you to weigh the advantages and disadvantages of these opportunities according to a spiritual perspective rather than jumping headlong into something because it seems to fulfill your immediate desire for material gain. These cards speak to your wisdom nature and ask you to think through your true desires for your life. They help you embrace a spiritual acceptance of abundance by acknowledging that abundance is only on loan to you from the Universe, the Earth, and/or Humanity. You are also put on notice that you are responsible in all of your choices for giving back more than you accrue for personal use. These are powerful and auspicious cards to draw, because they tell you that success is yours as you come to see that lasting abundance springs ultimately from an abundant heart and the love that is given without strings.

THE ANGELIC MESSENGER CARD SPREADS

Each card in the *Angelic Messenger Cards* divination system bears a number and a word that identifies a uniquely beautiful flower image selected specifically for the quality of spiritual energy it represents. The easiest way to locate the spiritual teaching applicable to a particular card is to refer to the number on the card and use this number to find the proper location in the *Angelic Messenger Cards* book. An exact black-and-white replica of the card you've chosen will always appear on the left-hand page in the book to allow you to confirm that you are reading the correct material. In order to gain the greatest benefit from the reading in the book, hold the individual full-color card that you've chosen directly over the black and white duplicate image as you read the symbolic interpretation and teaching for that card.

The *Angelic Messenger Cards* can be used in individual spreads or by drawing one card each day to complement and further enhance your other spiritual work.

Various spreads of cards are available to you to further your process of spiritual self-discovery and to increase your effectiveness in working with your angelic teachers: the "Opening to the Energy of Love" spread, the "Body-Mind-Spirit" spread, and the "Daily Guidance" spread. There are also effective ways to use the cards in connection with meditation.

The "Opening to the Energy of Love" Spread

This spread is meant to help you identify the most significant major issue or concern present in your life at this time, in each one of the six essential aspects of spiritual energy. You'll be able to consider these spiritual challenges as significant opportunities, as important doorways, for your work right now in your quest for greater spiritual awareness and understanding.

To organize the cards into this spread, separate them into the six categories or qualities of spiritual energy. In other words, place all *Reflection* Cards (Numbers 1–7) in one group, all *Partnership* Cards (Numbers 8–14) in another group, and so forth, until you have six stacks of seven cards each. You may also divide the cards into their six groups according to the different colors shown in the card numbers. The numbers that are printed in purple, for example, correspond to the cards of *Reflection*, the numbers in red are *Partnership*, those in orange are *Integration*, and so on. The remaining six cards from your deck are wild cards and consist of four *Divine Guid-ance* cards and two *Abundance* cards. Set the wild cards aside; they are not needed for use in this spread.

To use this spread, shuffle or mix each of the six piles of cards in any way that you choose keeping the cards in each pile separate and face down. Then fan out each group of cards and intuitively choose one card from each of the six groups. The sequence in which you choose from each group does not matter. Before choosing, hold in your heart the intention of selecting the cards most appropriate for you at this time.

This spread is best used when you have time to absorb all the guidance you will receive, such as on a quiet day at home, while on vacation, or over a long weekend. It is very useful as a base-line evaluation when you first begin your work with The *Angelic Messenger Cards* and at periodic intervals there-after. Much like a physical x-ray, the guidance you receive spiritually from the "Opening to the Energy of Love" spread gives you a means of evaluating your progress in matters that are not so easily measured but are the crucial basis for your health and well-being.

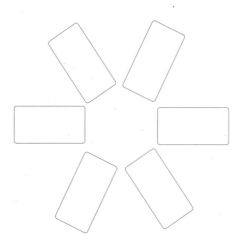

The "Body-Mind-Spirit" Spread

To use this spread, shuffle the entire deck of cards, including wild cards, and then spread the deck out in a fan shape, with the flower images face down. Hold within you the quiet inner intention of finding insight into ways to deal with, understand, and/or respond to a special concern or question you have. Run your hands slowly and lightly over the cards and intuitively choose three cards.

These three cards together offer you guidance for merging your inner and outer energies and for the integration of your body, mind, and spirit that is required now in order for you to complete your present level of spiritual work and to improve your physical well-being.

Use the "Body-Mind-Spirit" spread when you are seeking to heal your physical body or overcome a serious loss that is hampering your inner movement. Ask to be shown or taught in the most appropriate way, so that you can accept and learn from the substantial changes being asked of you at this important moment in your life.

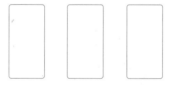

The "Daily Guidance" Spread

To use this spread, shuffle all the cards together including the wild cards, and then spread them out in a fan shape in front of you. Allow the strength of your need or desire for guidance and answers to a particular question to form the energy that flows out from your heart through your fingertips and permits you to sense the most appropriate card. Choose the card that seems to want to come into your fingers. You will find the exact card you need.

If you want further explanation or a different vantage point for your specific concern, question, or need, then draw a second card, and combine your insights from the two readings in your *Angelic Messenger Cards* book. You may also draw a second additional card for an even deeper perspective on your question or concern.

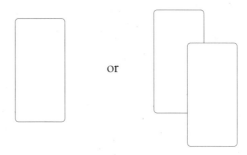

or

Meditation to Invoke Abundance in Your Life

If you are especially worried or concerned about a financial situation or are in immediate need of any level of abundance, pull out the *Abundance* wild card from the deck and read the teaching offered in The *Angelic Messenger Cards* book for that card. Then place both hands on the open pages of the book, over the words you've just read, and close your eyes, invoking all the genuine power of the reading to flow directly into your life. Keep the original card with you during the day or over the next several weeks until your situation has found a resolution. You can work with this card in addition to your normal daily work with the other cards.

Meditation to Invoke Divine Guidance in Your Life

If you need the Universe's direct help in an emergency or feel particularly urgent about needing to reach God, follow the same procedure as with the *Abundance* wild card, only meditate upon invoking divine guidance in your life. This card enhances your energy field, especially in your call to be heard by the angels and teachers of the light.

Getting the Most from the Angelic Messenger Cards & Flowers

Resist the temptation to read the materials as if you are reading a cook book. You are reading words that are meant to pick up on the subtlest of inner shifts and to trigger your own spirit's emerging energy. This means luxuriating in the words and thoughts in an unhurried fashion. Keep a journal or note pad next to you as you read, so that the precious and fleeting glimpses of insight that you're receiving while reading this material can be written down and considered separately in other meditations.

Each time you draw a particular card you will find something important urging itself upon you. Even if at the first reading you aren't sure how the material relates to your life, read it again, but with less of a practical or absolute idea of what the material is saying. Spiritual work is often the realization that a new impression comes much as does the fragrance of a fine wine, by being savored upon the tongue before being swallowed.

The thoughts and message occurring to you in between and around the thoughts you actually read are as important as, or even more important than, the actual printed message on the page. You will draw those cards you need to awaken your inner messages from your angelic messengers.

UNDERSTANDING THE FOUR SECTIONS OF MATERIAL FOR EACH CARD

The guidance for each card is organized into four sections: Present Challenge, Angelic Message, Spiritual Opportunity, and Application. Each of these four sections has a specific purpose, a special part to play in your understanding of the angelic message brought you by the card.

Present Challenge

The present challenge helps you identify what you feel as the undercurrents that have caused you to draw this card. This challenge may be obvious to you, or you may need to think about it before you discover your own interpretation of this challenge. You can trust your own intuition and the fact that you have drawn this card for a specific reason relating to your effectiveness in the world and your own spiritual advancement.

Angelic Message

This is a message from the angels brought through the angelic presence of Mentor, an advanced teacher, whose focus and attention is on raising the inner spiritual energy of individuals on the Earth at this time.

The guidance offered in this section is meant to expand your understanding of the message from a larger, more insightful perspective. The Angelic message can be read and re-read because something significant is always ready to be seen with each new reading. Writing that is drawn from the wisdom mind of master teachers and avatars of the Universe is always given in layers of understanding. As we peel away one layer, the next level appears to us even though we are reading the same words.

Spiritual Opportunity

This section interprets the flower image on the card you have drawn. The *Angelic Messenger Cards* set is meant to help you better understand the messages of the angels by heightening your perception through symbolic interpretation of the flower images. The message reflected from the angels through the flower image chosen has something significant for your own growth that day, to help you in many ways to be more successful and peaceful with your life.

Application

This section offers specific ways in which the message of the card can be further integrated and understood. These include exercises and practical things to do, think about, and work with in order to better absorb the teaching offered on this subject from the angels.

EXPECT TO RECEIVE THE APPROPRIATE GUIDANCE

There is no right or wrong way to learn from these cards. You are being directed along a spiritual path that has as its basis love and compassion for all living things. In whatever ways you are growing in truth, you are where you should be. Because you are being taught truth, you will gradually come to appreciate the inner freedom emerging from your heart as you find the way to step through the world of mere rational/intellectual interpretation and use your intuition to awaken a deeper guidance.

When you are being encouraged and helped to understand that the Universe is equally concerned with each being and each living thing, you permit judgement, criticism, arrogance, and self-importance to fall away. You will find you no longer need recognition of your ego in the same way. Rather, you will be able to accept your value without needing either to verify your value or to undervalue yourself in the eyes of the world.

A gentle and awake heart is the best climate in which to accept spiritual truths. As we are enabled to shift the command of our lives increasingly to our spirits, we are released from the incessant strain of experiencing physical and emotional woes. We become enlightened, capable of holding and experiencing the light of Divine Love.

The Universe seems to be easing us into greater and greater acceptance of a far-reaching universal spirituality that we touch only as we have the courage to reach for personal God-realization. Gossamer veils are all that separate the physical and spiritual realities, and even these obstructions seem to be falling away as we are pushed to grow spiritually. We hope to leave a healthier planet to our children, one that has benefited from our passing this way. In order to do this we are urged by the Universe to seek our own true identity—the reason we came to the Earth—and to live it now.

Use the *Angelic Messenger Cards* in good heart and with joy. And as you do, the true benefits of spirit will grace your inner journey always.

CONTINUING YOUR WORK WITH FLOWERS

As you find greater and greater pleasure and meaning in working with The *Angelic Messenger Cards*, you may want to work with live flowers to find the answers to specific questions and to further define your life.

Guidance isn't difficult to hear, but it does take an ability to listen from an inner space that is different from reading the words on a page, for instance, or listening to someone's voice. Guidance is a perceptual experience that requires the ability to explore imagery, symbology, and archetypal images to help you find a framework into which you can fit the day's guidance. Guidance involves allowing a wide variety of images, disconnected feelings, and thoughts to flow unobstructed through your mind. The exact interpretation of these sensations will fall into place on its own, much the way a ball on a roulette wheel revolves around and around but eventually falls into a slot. So, too, will your guidance become clear as the pieces fall together appropriately.

Take the first step to open this door of angelic guidance by choosing a flower that feels good to you today. If you are going to pick one to bring inside, always ask it first to withdraw its energy back to the Earth and its essence. Always appreciate it for growing and for offering you the opportunity to walk your own path more clearly. It doesn't matter if you buy a cut flower or choose a potted plant. Artificial flowers, on the other hand, may be beautiful, but they carry no energy. So the flower you work with must be alive.

After choosing a flower as your angelic messenger, close your eyes and take a deep breath. Steady your breathing with several regular breaths. Then open your eyes and look into the flower you are holding. The angelic message for you is just in this moment, in this day. It is relevant to you because of your willingness to accept the teaching of the Universe, of your own angelic teachers and masters.

WHAT TO LOOK FOR IN GUIDANCE FROM FLOWERS

Your powers of observation and introspection are essential in gleaning guidance from flowers. Select one particular plant and first notice the nature of the growth and the way in which an individual blossom develops from it. Are you observing the blossom as a bud, beginning to open, fully open, or moving past its peak, with the petals beginning to fade and fall off? Is there more than one bud or blossom on the stalk? How do you feel about your own life at this moment? Are you the bud just beginning to claim your destiny in the world? Are you the full-blown flower, living life completely? What color is the flower? Is it all one color or a fusion of several colors? Does one color slide gradually into another hue? Is your life sliding into a more profound state or into a more relaxed and sublime understanding? You will choose a particular flower for a reason. Remember that all you read into it has direct, specific, and important meaning and reassurance for you.

Now look inside the flower. See if you can see the pistil, or seed-bearing center section of the flower. Are you bearing any new seeds of desired change in your life? What feelings come to mind as you look at the stamen, the pollen-bearing spears that surround the center seed pod? What are you probing or protecting? The thoughts that come to you are inspired thoughts, filled with the musings of the angels. You are being shown, talked to, held, supported, and loved.

Look at the petals next. Are they held tightly as in a bud, reflecting unrealized potential? Are they relaxed fully, suggesting an accepting and believing attitude about life? Is there a sharp contrast between the position of the petals and the inner pistil and stamen?

Each time you accept guidance through one of these angelic messengers, it will be different. The guidance coming to you isn't static and pat, but unique, individualized and appropriate for this very moment of your life and for this very question to which you seek an answer.

Life is in abundance all around us, and the flowers symbolically show us the reflection of God. All our anxieties can find reassurance as we accept the blessings of the angels. We are guided with each breath we take, and through each heartfelt gaze into a flower we do indeed hear the voices of the angels.

Colors and the Qualities they Represent

purple—spiritual intention or involvement
pink—love, compassion
red—intense feelings, passion, action
orange—balance, inner and/or outer
yellow—intellectual or rational thinking
gold—divine awareness, spiritual healing
greeen—physical and emotional healing, drawing from nature
blue—serenity, peacefulness
brown—stability, groundedness
white—perfection, angelic/divine involvement
black—release, rebirth, and transformation

Angelic Messenger Cards

Love

I

Love

PRESENT CHALLENGE
Seeking clarity through spiritual awareness.

You have drawn this card of Love to help you make important decisions for your life, create clarity out of confusion, and move through ambivalence and daily struggle.

You may feel that the choices you are being asked to make seem too hard and the solutions too obscure. You may feel unprepared to do what life seems to be leading you toward and that the problems you face are too complex to even solve and/or that depression and unsettledness are becoming too-familiar emotional and spiritual companions. All these feelings may also be mixed with a sense of impatience, an impression that you are ready to create the life you want but that the means of achieving or uncovering this new direction seem obscured.

ANGELIC MESSAGE
Love

We are calling to you to sort through your life and to find new or more meaningful means of nurturing yourself, surrounding yourself with people who love and respect you. Seeking spiritual awareness, the emergence of love within, is a hollow enterprise unless you can see each and every thought and action as contributing to the transformation of life already underway within you. Your true potential and power through love are mere shadows unless you recognize that love is the process that, used daily, will draw the right people and the most beneficial opportunities into your life.

Loving yourself and finding goodness in others will help you achieve specific goals. You are being encouraged to expect love in your life and in all your relationships as the means through which you will learn the easiest.

Love in your heart will help you assess those tasks that you truly want to perform and that will bring you meaningful and purposeful growth. Your life is leading you toward a deeper connection with the divine Source, and all those daily practices that encourage this deeper penetration of the divine Essence will be encouraged.

Assume that you are journeying toward enlightenment and that you are seeking to expand your spirit and your access to the dimension of divine Love that heals. You are being guided to breathe into and breathe through each problem, accepting the truth that you are learning the means to discriminate between those people and means of living that support your enlightenment and those that represent only detours. You are learning the means to separate truth from illusion in your life and in your expectations. Move out of unnecessary action and busy-ness. Find opportunities for quiet times, and reflect on the profound life changes underway in your life.

You are loved more than you can imagine, and we the angels of all life are emerging into your presence so that you can draw from our love and re-merge with the essence of God from which you originated.

SPIRITUAL OPPORTUNITY

The flower displayed to you on this card, a luscious, fuchsia-colored blossom, is fully present to its inner cycles. The guidance that comes to you through this image is to become equally cognizant of your inner being and more fully available emotionally and spiritually to the learning inherent in each day.

You have drawn this card because you are ready to accept that you no longer need to be, or feel, overwhelmed by life's demands or by the lack of clear direction or focus for your future. You are in a spiritual clarification phase, and you are being called to accept that at this time your future is unfolding spiritually more than intellectually.

With this card you are being guided to have more faith in your intuitive choices and unexpressed initiatives. Like the yet-unopened bud in the center of this flower, with its surrounding dark definition, you are seeking to realize your emerging potential. You are coming back into love with yourself so that you can be with others in ways that are more supportive and comforting and so that you can expect the same from others. Try to be patient with yourself and realize that your present circumstances are important steppingstones on your spiritual journey.

APPLICATION

This is a time when many small and insignificant chores and commitments will seem to eat into the time you want to spend with your partner, children, or close friends. Learn that you are not required to be all things to all people. You are within the energy flow of love that says you can love others enough to say "no." You do have sufficient time to accomplish essential tasks if you allow others to share in the creation and implementation of plans. You can attract the financial resources you need as you realize that love is energy and it promotes a natural state of abundance and well-being. You can use acceptance of yourself as the means to awaken love and the meaningful guidance that can bring you greater comfort and solace.

Wholeness

2

Wholeness

PRESENT CHALLENGE
Rediscovering and/or deepening your commitment to your spiritual nature.

You have drawn this card because you may be tired of people pushing you to be different from the way you are—either more sensitive or more assertive, or more reflective of what others think you should be. While you are certainly changing and seeking to learn from others, you also need to understand the strengths of your own nature.

This card is encouraging you so you will recognize that you may be using your skill and creativity in ways that keep others from seeing your true worth. You may be quiet and excessively shy, or you may be the first to see the solution or to offer others a means of solving a problem. You may need to heed others' feelings about your efforts in order to modify your own natural way of being rather than trying to change it.

ANGELIC MESSAGE
Wholeness

Wholeness is more a state of spirit than a state of mind. When you were a child you assumed you were entirely perfect until others told you that you were not. The challenge of finding wholeness in your life today is in recognizing that this latent sense of joyful understanding is still within you and needs to be brought forth into your life.

Your purpose in this lifetime, a purpose now manifesting into actual activity, is based on learning to believe in the guidance of your spirit. You can truly gain self-assurance only through inner assurance, and that comes from rediscovering the joy you once knew. This joy came from union with the Divine.

When we shepherded you into your mother's womb, you were sure you would never forget us, your angelic guardians. You were committed to your upcoming physical life as an expression of your love for all living things. You were coming to Earth for specific spiritual reasons, and you knew what these were. Now is the time to remember and recapture these early insights, because you need more confidence, a feeling that arises from your own inner knowledge. This is a time for accelerated growth, and we are ready to again remind you of your choices and leanings. You are ready for deeper levels of responsibility, for the Earth is in need of healing.

Each human being seeks to re-merge with the peace and joy of those early moments of life. You are experiencing the desire to live your vision as completely as possible. The only way to do this is to follow the lifeline of your years on the Earth back to the early days when you began this living adventure and when you knew your life mission.

SPIRITUAL OPPORTUNITY

Observe the profoundly simple but elegant nature of the gorgeous purple blossom on the card that has come to you. This blossom has a specific purpose, just as your life does. The flower has an inner focus—sharp and profoundly golden. Gold is the color of ultimate healing and God-awareness. Nothing clutters this flower's intention; it sends its beauty and fragrance into the world unfettered by anything other than its own unique presence. With this card you are being guided to be clear, straightforward, and inspired by the God within.

This is the time to begin new projects, to expand your horizons, because you accept that God is at work within you. You are moving under the energy of growth and opportunity, and your spirit is supporting your efforts in every way. You may feel this inner movement as bursts of unexpected energy, sudden shifts in your mood, momentary realizations that give you a clear picture of some problem you've been trying to solve.

New awareness and a stronger intuitive perceptiveness go along with this energy of wholeness. This card comes to suggest that you can find wholeness because you are really ready to release the past and genuinely committed to creating a different future for yourself, for those you love, and/or for the Earth and all other living things.

APPLICATION

Start afresh each morning with the resolve to enjoy the best of the day, to listen most intently to the comments from others that are positive and that offer you something worthwhile to consider. Release and let slip away any other comments or remarks that are critical or dampening to your spirit and that feel perplexing.

Give yourself personal spiritual tasks to complete, like filling out a short list of the five most important spiritual qualities that you admire; then ask yourself to comment on what these mean to you and in what way you exemplify these qualities.

Consider starting each morning with a prayer of appreciation for the opportunity for life; follow each noontime meal with a prayer of gratitude for the wisdom you have received and are about to use; and draw each day to a close with a prayer of acceptance of the love that has come to you from the Divine.

Expansiveness

3

Expansiveness

PRESENT CHALLENGE
***Setting aside your intellectual beliefs and awakening
your intuitive wisdom.***

This card of Reflection is asking you to expand your understanding of God. You may have fallen into a pattern of believing that God functions as a person does, and so you are bewildered, wondering why a loving God would let terrible things happen to innocent people in your life or elsewhere on the Earth.

You have drawn this card to expand your awareness and to increase your understanding and perception of the Divine. With this card you are being challenged to release old patterns and to discover a divine Source you may be less familiar with. This card alerts you that a new level of deep intuitive wisdom is emerging into your consciousness and that you are being asked to suspend judgement and to pay attention to the events unfolding in your life because they are meant to teach you.

ANGELIC MESSAGE
Expansiveness

We come to share with you the realization that you have outgrown your belief system: God is more than you are imagining. The time has come for you to re-create God, using the fullest expanse of your imagination. Even if you do this, you will still under-imagine God. There is no separation between you and the Divine or between you and your neighbor, or between you and our angelic kingdom. There is also no division within you or any other living thing, and there is no good or evil as separate forces. Both aspects of God are but mirror images of the other, and both fit within the grand design of God.

In order to find yourself, you need to look within the all-encompassing divine Presence. To understand your relationship with God, you need to unlearn the concept of separation and substitute the reality of expansiveness from one common source (God). To find God you are required to go deep within, way beneath any prior learning about God, to experience for yourself the intricacy and expansiveness of life itself.

You may have formed your opinions about the Divine on the basis of what you've read, learned, and observed. All these impressions are merely the thoughts, feelings, and judgements of other individuals who, like yourself, are also searching. Because you've chosen this lifetime to come to know God better, your wisdom is as true as that of others when you seek the wisdom that is your spiritual core. You are awakening to a new life, and this change requires an additional realization of your own true divine Nature. You can benefit from observing God in action—through the intricate beauty and presence of the flowers.

SPIRITUAL OPPORTUNITY

The guidance that comes to you through this flower is to reclaim your divine right to love and to abundance and, in return, to use these forms of energy as does the Divine: as the basis for all creation. This golden flower seeks to entice you into the unknown. The purpose laid out for you now in your life is to set aside decisions and judgements and to journey deep within to determine the meaning of your existence. All else will wait while you refocus the Sacred in your life.

Expansiveness is a state of being that carries you deeply

into the realm of your spirit by means of past learned or experienced limitations. The portals of awareness beckon to you just as the golden light of the flower opens to some deeper inner truth. What is your own inner truth, and in what way does it lead to your own purpose and sustenance?

As you undertake this journey inward, you awaken your spiritual energy, and it eases you through old, limiting boundaries. Others may feel antagonized or threatened by your focus on life as a spiritual process. Keep aligned with your own truth, because this card is telling you that as you seek to redefine your own values and your relationship with God, you are protected on your spiritual journey. Look for the presence of love and divine affection in every face you see today. Trust your own intuition, and seek to develop your spirit by taking ten minutes out of every hour to see the divine Presence within your life in some way.

APPLICATION

If God is beyond definition, then in what way can you understand Him/Her/It? You've drawn this card of Reflection to help you reflect upon God's nature. In order to become love, you are required not to define it but to experience it. Try experiencing God as something you do, use, invoke, and accept that brings you and others joy and inner peace.

Look down at your hands and realize that they are of God, the movement is of God, the fingernails and hangnails are also of God. Likewise, the rings you wear, the color of your skin, and the life-force that allows you to respond to your brain's signals to move your fingers on command, are of God. When you thus experience God you can live in this light without any fear.

Awareness

4

Awareness

PRESENT CHALLENGE
Gaining spiritual insight as you release past emotional pain.

You have drawn this card to further awaken your spirit and to help you feel safe as you break through past limitations. You may feel dulled by life and longing for a peak spiritual experience that will assure you of your path.

This card is coming to you to say that spiritual growth is a process and that plateaus are present at all stages of spiritual work. Feeling stalled may indicate that you are still absorbing the learning available from a recent significant change in your life. Feeling glued to your present state of ennui or lassitude may also indicate that you need to accept the nature of normal day-to-day spiritual practice.

ANGELIC MESSAGE
Awareness

Your entire life has a focus, and this focus is at your center, the center of your being, which is your spirit or inner mind. Your essential self is given the work of discovering itself, and this is the journey through life. You may wonder why it is that you seem to have come into this life having had this essential knowledge erased.

It would seem so much easier to be able to recognize inherently the differences between impulses arising from the Divine and those arising as coping mechanisms for life.

We, your angelic teachers, suggest that your essential knowledge has not been erased, merely implanted deep within you so that you must search in the right ways to discover it. The Divine is seen in everything and every way. You cannot go to the store, eat a meal, pat your family dog, or sleep in the arms of your lover without knowing the God within you. Likewise, you cannot hear of the death of a friend, say good-bye to your children as they head into the world, leave a job, or break your leg and not know God. God is the totality of your living experience.

Your journey into awareness is to imagine that everything you eat, think, touch, and absorb every day is somehow teaching you about God. Your desire to become aware of God is providing the impetus for your recognition of the Divine that is constantly at work in your life. As you realize that you are an inseparable part of God, you want to know more of the ways to accept this realization. When you meditate, you have the opportunity to accept God into your heart because you are accepting your own divine nature. This acceptance allows a subtle but life-shifting merger to take place. Awareness of your acceptance encourages merger with the Divine, and this merger is the pathway to enlightenment.

SPIRITUAL OPPORTUNITY

The guidance through the flower that appears on this card tells you that you are emerging through past pain, loss, fear, rejection, or abuse to assume a more dramatic and visible means of working to heal other living things. You are entering a powerful time of spiritual insight because of your desire to learn from past negative experiences. Your healing capacity is being awakened, and you may discover that more advanced levels of spiritual insight are becoming available to you. You may discover, for instance, skill in clairaudience or clairvoyance, or in running healing energy through your hands. These abilities are a natural outgrowth of your return to the wisdom of your basic spiritual nature.

You can easily imagine this card as speaking to you from the angels because of the soft, creamy color of the petals and the green, healing energy of the center or heart of the flower. This flower is suggesting that you, too, will benefit from becoming or remaining soft and receptive, seeking to receive love continually from the Universe as the basis for your healing work. This flower image carries an extremely positive energy for transformation into new levels of insight and work. Be sure not to underestimate your worth or ability to maximize upcoming opportunities. This card tells you to be aware of subtle influences and not to discount whatever comes to you, because it offers you opportunities to reclaim your true inner power.

APPLICATION

You are part of the subtle energy field of the entire Universe and are thus able to sense life force in other people and such livings things as animals, plants, and trees. Practice sensing the movement of these subtle currents of life within other living systems. Cup your hands around a beautiful flower, for instance; close your eyes, and allow your angels to guide your thoughts. Try opening your eyes and talking directly into the flower, sharing your daily concerns, expectations, needs, and dreams. Talking to a specific flower each day is an especially effective way to awaken dialogue with your angels and to hear their guidance for you.

Willpower

5

Willpower

PRESENT CHALLENGE
Finding the inner discipline to stay consistent with your daily spiritual practices.

You have drawn this card of Willpower to alert you that the quality and time spent in your spiritual work and study needs to be re-evaluated. This card suggests that you require a more direct relationship with the Divine so that you can feel more aligned throughout your daily activities.

You may be feeling uneasy about your meditations and the time you spend in prayer. You may feel stalled, or perhaps stale, in your inner work. You may be questioning the effectiveness of your spiritual practices. You may also be aware that you are easily distracted, that your life seems too busy for finding adequate time to meditate, and/or that you have no quiet place in which you can be alone. You may feel also that it is time to take the next step to deepen your relationship with God. This card is asking you to consider your means for growing spiritually.

ANGELIC MESSAGE
Willpower

To have willpower seems to be considered difficult, fraught with struggle, and a desire to be somewhere else doing something other

*than what has been undertaken. Does the flower need willpower to
seek the sun? Does the flower need willpower to hold the raindrop?
Do you need willpower to know your divine essence?*

*Being in alignment with God is the purpose of existence, so how
can it be so difficult? Is willpower, then, an act of ultimate contri-
tion, the performance of a difficult and unwanted task? The divine
love of the Universe doesn't need willpower to find you; it simply
runs along the currents of your life and merges with you as you let
it. The flower allows the natural elements of its life to co-exist
within its petals and stem. The Universe is freely found when you
have the desire to look at what is fully present and easily seen
through the mystery and beauty of physical existence. Pain and
sorrow, like all paths, lead to the Divine.*

*Love isn't found by using willpower. Spiritual practice that is
enlightening and important to your life isn't found with willpower
but rather with the encouragement of your soul. You create a disci-
plined spirit from desire to know God, and it is this energy that
merges your heart's desire with the force of your ego to create a
powerful antidote for the pressures of your daily living.*

SPIRITUAL OPPORTUNITY

This card is suggesting that you have entered a time of shifting energies and that success and positive growth comes from
staying centered within the quiet focus of divine love. The
guidance it offers is to remain focused on your daily work with
spirit. The dewdrop falls naturally to the center of the flower
just as the essence of divine love moves of its own natural
accord to your own inner center of spirit. This center is the
place of all successful growth, change, and progress.

Your life is presently similar to the graceful flower petals
that sway, bend, and twist in the force of physical circumstances. The people and circumstances in your life are undergoing change, and through this flower you are being guided to
stay balanced within your own center so that you are not
thrown out of alignment and away from your purpose by the

shifts that others are making. You are being offered the wisdom of the still point, placing your trust and belief in your own nature as it is aligned with the forces of Providence.

APPLICATION

Meditation is an essential part of self-exploration. When you sit to meditate, try relaxing your upper body so that you can sway back and forth or from side to side, or you can move your shoulders, your neck, or your head. Movement helps hold the mind's attention and thus gives you added insight into and access to the non-verbal aspects of your subconscious and superconscious. When you are excited and intrigued by the results you are getting from your meditation, then it ceases to be a drudgery and becomes the most interesting and significant part of your day.

Use the daily routines of your day to practice the awareness you've been given in meditation by your angelic teachers. Whether or not you feel you have a direct angelic interaction, assume that the questions you pose in meditation are receiving attention from your teachers. The effect of any learning from the nonphysical world is to improve your ability to be a loving and compassionate person on the Earth. As you see inner movement in this direction, assume you are being guided.

Blessing

6

Blessing

PRESENT CHALLENGE
Seeing the blessings in your life.

Reflection cards all lead you more deeply inside yourself so that you can rediscover your own spirit and the means of living in an awakened relationship with God/The Source.

This card brings you the message that the blessings of your life can sustain you even when you or someone you love is in great distress and pain. By focusing on the blessings that your spirit has brought to you or to another, you are better able to learn from the difficulties in your life rather than seeking only to survive them. This card offers renewal and increased self-appreciation because it asks you to lift your eyes from the mundane and fearful toward the evolved and enlightened.

ANGELIC MESSAGE
Blessing

Have you ever wondered what allows someone to have a thankful heart? Each person alive today would like to have a positive, loving attitude and outlook, but some find it almost impossible to set down their weariness in order to find the blessings in their lives.

A blessing is an actual thing. A blessing carries the love from the

Universe directly into your heart. If you are waiting to know bless-
ings with your mind, you will wait forever, because blessings are
recognized only through the heart, inner mind, or spirit.

A blessing is divine realization manifested in a meaningful and
recognizable way. A blessing is an open invitation to understand
more, a gentle loving essence to sustain and hold you when you are
hurt, a magical awareness of some truth that you had forgotten or
never known before. A blessing is a gift of profound impact to your
heart, urging you to take a second look at life and to honor the
process of your living even if it is or has been painful and unpleas-
ant. Because your spirit can only love, it accepts blessings as the
natural kudos of life. Each blessing offers an awareness of grand
insight and wisdom for you to use as the basis of your own develop-
ing spiritual philosophy. Imagine the joy in your life if you had
heard and acknowledged every blessing that your spirit received
over all the years you've been alive. What would today be like for
you if you acknowledged the blessing or deeper loving intent offered
you through every relationship and unfolding circumstance? You
would quickly be a very joyful person.

SPIRITUAL OPPORTUNITY

This extraordinarily brilliant flower image is showing you the
nature of your life as it moves from the powerful purity of
divine awareness into the magical passion and intensity of
Earth-School life. You are being asked to see forthcoming success as the natural extension of continued attention to your
relationship with the divine Source. You are being blessed
with additional clarity and understanding of the past circumstances that have hindered your growth, and you can expect
to move ahead with plans to expand and grow.

Although the blessings of insight, inspiration, and integrity
are coming more fully into your life work and your relationships, you are being cautioned that as your future blossoms
you should continue to honor the small, daily blessings in
your life. Pay attention to the people, animals, plants, trees,

and natural systems that support your life. Pay attention to the seemingly unimportant people who support your success. The challenge is to realize that no matter how brilliant your future, how bright a star in the heavens you become, you are there by the grace of divine love. Your success is meant to help humanity and the Earth, and so your deepest intentions are being honored. Use the blessings in your own life to help others renew their belief in their own blessings from the Universe.

APPLICATION

Saying their prayers at night is a practice that many adults followed as children but failed to continue. Offering thanks and appreciation before meals is also a tradition that has slipped in many households. Practice these two important means of acknowledging the receipt of blessings into your life and the people close to you.

Try saying a grace in which each person contributes a word or thought. Try saying your prayers in ways that focus only on the blessings in your life rather than on what you still need in order to be happy or successful. Make a list of the people you love the most and the blessings that have come to you because of your relationship with each of these individuals. Then make a list of the people you dislike the most and the blessings that have come to you because of these relationships. How many blessings can you count in your life? In this one day? Before closing your eyes for the night, make a practice of mentally listing the blessings you've received that day.

Belief

7

Belief

PRESENT CHALLENGE
Harmonizing the duality of ego and spirit.

You've drawn this card to help yourself find internal harmony so that the person you truly believe yourself to be can emerge as the dominant role in your life.

Your anxiety over being loved, appreciated, and approved of, or your emotional investment in being different, being the rebel, or carrying on a solo act may be getting in the way of your opting for the choices you need to make and living in the way most conducive to your spiritual growth. This card is suggesting to you that you are underestimating your abilities and aptitudes because you observe your life skills primarily from the ego level. Your selection of this card suggests that you can benefit from observing your life from the spiritual dimension, where limitations are actually focused opportunities.

ANGELIC MESSAGE
Belief

When you are able to view, even for a few seconds, the beauty and loving nature of your inner mind or spirit, you recognize an inevitable split that lies at the basic level of your humanness. In

69

your mind dwells a duality that allows you to be two people and to operate with two vocabularies and belief systems at the same time. One belief system is associated with showing other people the ways in which you are proficient and important. The focus in this belief system is on getting your mental and emotional needs met. The other belief system has nothing to support or prove and wants only to remind you that you can live in peace, love, and genuine abundance by accepting your non-grasping self, your spirit. This second belief system focuses on helping you live in love and to believe enough in the power of this divine love that you are encouraged to respect yourself and all other living things.

In your meditations, as you seek to gain insight into your life and divine nature, you may ask to be more directly guided, held in a loving way, and instructed by the forces of Heaven so that you may find relief from the anguish of your life. We, your angelic teachers, suggest that you are being encouraged to redefine your life from the inside out, removing limitations and accepting your natural worth. As you cease fearing your reflection of divine intention and begin to place your focus directly on living your fullest essence, then you will learn from the guidance of many dimensions. Your mind and emotions are meant to reflect the beauty of your soul. When you live with the energy of love shining through your life, then you naturally have more confidence in yourself because this energy is a reflection of divine love.

SPIRITUAL OPPORTUNITY

The guidance from your angelic teachers through this flower image reinforces the power of the energy generated from the spiritual realm. While it may appear to you that the solutions to your life problems lie in changing only your attitudes, or in adjusting where, how, or in what place you live, this card is offering you a different perspective. With the choice of this card you are being assured that the changes you want to come about in your life will arise from a change in perception that releases you to live in ways that reflect your spiritual beliefs completely.

The flower's brightly-colored red petals with darker recesses represent the natural foil for your spiritual energy. Your spirit shines out, illuminating your life no matter the physical circumstances. This card is suggesting that you will find the most outer satisfaction by adjusting your inner beliefs. You are being required to seek God as the center to your life rather than as something tangential and taken for granted until you want or need something to be different.

APPLICATION

You are never upset for the reason you think you are. Finding the pressure point in your ego helps you understand that your ego's voice is different from your spirit's. The first step in self-exploration is to decide what you are exploring. Choose the first upset of the day, and ask your ego, "Why am I upset?" Write down your responses. Now ask yourself, "What do you, my spirit, have to teach me about my upset?" Write down your spirit's words, and use these as the standard for that day's living.

If you have trouble finding your spirit's voice, write out the second question above on a piece of paper. Then write your response to this question for ten minutes without lifting your pen. You'll find that, in spite of your ego's presence, you'll be able to delve more deeply into your inner self. This exercise of writing into your truth is valuable whenever you want greater insight and feel blocked from discovering it.

Potential

8

Potential

PRESENT CHALLENGE
Accepting yourself as your own "teacher," who can assess and create from your own spiritual intentions.

You have drawn this card of Partnership in order to expand your potential for joy, love, and creative expression. You may have felt for too long that others held the answers to your life or were responsible for blocking your progress. But now, through the circumstances unfolding in your life, you are reminded that you alone are required to make certain choices for your life and that in accepting this challenge you are awakening a level of creativity that for too long has laid dormant.

This card holds the energy of change and is alerting you to accept personal responsibility for the events that have unfolded in your past, to forgive others and move into your future with anticipation of success and joy. You have entered a period in which meaningful relationships will flow to you as you allow your creativity to reflect the wisdom of the Divine.

ANGELIC MESSAGE
Potential

God is the all-inclusive energy of divine love, and we, your angelic teachers, bring you the message that the fulfillment and joy you seek are but derivatives of this universal force. Nothing can stand in the way of your awakening to your potential except your own apathy, resistance, fear, or anxiety over finding your true relationship with the Divine.

God as energy encompasses both the light and the void, the joy of spiritual awakening and the pain produced by the void—the shadow self that emerges to obliterate your awareness of God's love. Both the light and the shadow have been vying for your attention, so your natural belief in yourself and your future may have been clouded temporarily by unforeseen circumstances. Potential is never diminished; only the confidence with which to use this natural spiritual creativity is ever damaged.

When you have faith that you are on the spiritual path, then the immediate circumstances in life are less anxiety-producing, and relationships can be built and also dismantled with less pain and trauma. You and all other people and living things have specific intentions for being on the Earth at this time. You are able to rest in the contentment of your own inner work with more assurance when you accept that God is within all the experiences presently or recently in your life: both the joy and the fear, both the searching and the discovery, both the enlightenment and the temporary loss of God's presence in your life.

Assume that you have a mission to accomplish that involves your own unique abilities. The world awaits your contributions. Put aside the voice of your ego-mind that tells you how to market yourself or your ability, and accept your spirit-mind, which tells you to use your natural creativity without thought for self-gain. Only through giving from your spiritual center will you truly realize and benefit from unleashing your potential.

SPIRITUAL OPPORTUNITY

The guidance to you through this card is a call to recognize that you, like this image, are also the bud. Even though you may have many accomplishments to your credit, your potential is still dormant. You have drawn this very important card of Partnership to encourage you to reassess the subtle dynamics of your closest relationships or partnership because you and perhaps others need to change the ways in which you've always interacted. You are also being alerted to the fact that others are unable to thwart your growth unless you believe that they can. You are responsible for living true to your own inner teachings and then working cooperatively with others in ways that encourage growth for all parties.

You are in a healing mode, with the color green facilitating your progress. The energy of growth and implied potential is coming to you with this card to tell you to give yourself and those closest to you permission to grow from the bud into the blossom. Important and essential spiritual growth is trying to emerge into your life, and you are being urged to grow from the "student" into the "teacher." Taking this step in awareness requires you to put your full attention on the state of your own spiritual health and well-being and to acknowledge your own guidance.

APPLICATION

Make a list of the spiritual qualities you associate with the bud—the student—and also with the full-blown flower—the teacher. Does it feel safer to be the bud because the student is not expected to know, to perform, or to assume responsibility for fully engaging his or her potential?

Bring a small flowering plant into your house or your office. Watch it grow from the bud stage into its fullness. Imagine that you also are changing and growing as quickly and with as much certainty of the rightness of your choices as this flower does. Seek to hear your guidance daily from the flowers.

Tenderness

9

Tenderness

PRESENT CHALLENGE
Developing more meaningful communication with those you love and work with.

You have drawn this card to guide you toward more effective and intuitive communication with others. You have come to a time when you are being urged to release old influences that keep you preoccupied in conversation or in unnecessarily defensive and protective statements of your own view or ideas. This card is meant to help you put aside your past and to accept a different future.

This may be a time of rapid change in relationships with those close to you. You are entering an important process of spiritual growth in which celebration of life is required, and so your relationships are needing to become lighter, more playful, and less ponderous but at the same time capable of greater depth. With this card you are being guided to hold your own counsel and to proceed from inner power.

ANGELIC MESSAGE
Tenderness

Tenderness is a profound spiritual quality embodying the deepest and most essential ingredients in lasting relationships. Tenderness speaks to a suppleness of spirit, flexibility in moving, shifting, and accepting different opinions and objectives, and recognition of one's physical finiteness and the opposite as one's spiritual immortality.

Tenderness is present in any bonding between people because it acknowledges the inevitable human struggle for life and happiness along with an acceptance that in the end all things die to be reborn. Tenderness awakens your deepest compassion. It also helps you trust others because you and they accept that dialogue is meant to encourage and shape rather than to tear down or undermine.

You have entered a decade of rapid and dramatic change, and in order for your relationships to withstand these sweeping energy shifts, two factors will need to be held firmly in your awareness. First, you are responsible for communicating from the values and knowledge held by your spirit rather than only from your mind and emotions. Second, your spirit holds the truth of your existence. If you learn to listen to it, you will be able to hear your own emotional needs and at the same time act in alignment with your spirit.

Relationships change at the spiritual level before noticeably changing on the emotional level. Long before a person breaks out of any sort of relationship, he or she has learned or felt something deeply true that has not been honored or expressed. Communication that lifts the spirit is based on acknowledgment of life as a spiritual process.

Relationships are metamorphosing as people awaken to their inner spiritual perspectives and values. People come together today to help their spirits mirror a primordial wisdom that comes from deep within. Relationships are joyful and important to your life only when they enhance or shift your own inner wisdom. For this to happen you need to trust, value, and respect those you enter relationships with, or you will be unable to accomplish your spiritual mission.

SPIRITUAL OPPORTUNITY

The guidance through this flower can help you observe and learn from the contrast and complementarity of your inner and outer natures. This lovely flower image shows you its own difference between its outer presence—or, symbolically, the face it shows to the world—and its inner nature—the divinely-inspired essence. The flower's external color of pink represents love and guides you to appreciate the importance of giving and receiving love in your life. The inner image of white symbolizes divine perfection and is set off by pinpoints of crimson, which represent moments of bliss, meaningful guidance, and interaction with the Divine and the universal teachers. This image is a metaphor for your life and the continuity that is possible when your life reflects tenderness.

APPLICATION

This card urges you to create a new language with your partner or others close to you. You need to recognize that you and your spouse/child/parent is trying to tell you something by his or her remarks, actions, and/or assumed inability or unwillingness to meet your needs adequately. Assume that when your needs are unmet, so are those of the other persons.

Ask those close to you to participate in creating meaningful ground rules that apply to arguments and misunderstandings. Consider such practices as always using the first person ("I" or "me") when speaking. Refuse to accept that one person is right and the other wrong. Speak your truth while at the same time accepting that others will see their truth more easily than yours. Believe in yourself enough to ask others to hear what you need to say. Setting up a shared personal language for relationships allows you and others to express your feelings and your beliefs while at the same time making room for others to also be as right and as sure of their opinions as you are.

Passion

10

Passion

PRESENT CHALLENGE:
Allowing passion to grow from compassion.

You have drawn this card in order to translate and transform feelings of frustration, anger, stagnation, close-down, or fear associated with intimacy. You may also have drawn this card to expand your understanding of sexuality so that your partnership/relationship with others can develop deeper spiritual channels.

You may want a different level of intimacy but feel others are to blame for your lack of it. You may feel frustrated and even bitter that others have relationships while you do not. You may feel lonely, distant from those with partners, and/or disappointed in the quality of your present relationship(s). Or you may wonder whether a new relationship would be different from or better than your present one. This card is meant to help you claim the passion already present in your life.

ANGELIC MESSAGE
Passion

Humanity's attraction to intimacy is a spiritual call to bring forth divine compassion for all life and to bless the beginnings and endings of the cycles of all living things. Divine compassion is experi-

enced as sexuality and spirituality, the mingling of the energy of the physical and the spiritual. These two entwined energies represent the ever-present and essential force of nature at work and the eternal force of spirit forever seeking renewal.

You are entering a period in the evolution of your species that requires a renewal and restabilization of spiritual energy as the natural balance to physical contact and emotional interplay. Sexual intimacy is possible when sacred overtones are in place and when procreation or enjoyment is the result of personal acceptance of love-making as a joyful and compassionate spiritual process. Expressed in this way, sexuality can help you release loneliness, discover joy and mutual expression of bliss, and recognize divine love being drawn into your heart.

Your passion is part of your compassion. Without compassion you can have no passion, for the one grows from the other. Spiritual compassion means reflecting on the presence of the Divine and seeing this image in all other living things, including your partner and other close relationships. Passion is heightened energy, and the release of this energy validates the goodness of the human experience. Your ability to love and enjoy the true nature of your relationship is thus the genuine goal of the merger of sexuality and spirituality. Passion gives rise to genuine intimacy.

SPIRITUAL OPPORTUNITY

The guidance coming to you through this flower image is meant to confirm your need for passion, both physical and spiritual, in your life and to assure you that it is natural to intensely desire to spread your seed—meaning the insight and wisdom you've gleaned—to others in this world.

This guidance is suggesting that you may not always have a partner who suits your physical needs and yet you always have a partner, or had a partner or close friend, that suited your spiritual needs at the time. If you are in a partnership that seems incomplete, unsatisfying, and without joy, then you are being called to find the passion in your own life. If you are without a partner, you are also being called to find the passion in your own life. If you are in a meaningful relationship with one special person or several close friends, then you are again being called to find the passion in your own life.

Passion is the feeling and presence of joy that arises when considering a challenge that you agree to accept. You have drawn this card of Partnership to encourage you to find the passion within your life by re-directing your energy away from confrontation and blame or simple dissipation through stress and preoccupation. You are being called to reinvest your energy and passion in your own spiritual choices and life opportunities. It takes passion to attract passion, and it takes personal spiritual responsibility to work on personal issues while at the same time creating a meaningful and safe forum for exchange with your partner and/or close friends.

APPLICATION

Are you always hard on yourself, thinking the worst of your motives and actions? Is it difficult for you to "catch yourself" engaging in these all-too-familiar destructive patterns? Are you ready to be loved and respected and to have a partner who honors your true worth and/or continues to grow with you?

Create a new message to play within your mind. Give yourself permission to be right rather than wrong, optimistic rather than pessimistic, hopeful rather than fearful, accepting of your life and your motives, and willing to be responsible for changing. Place the words "passion" and "compassion" in places where you'll have time to reflect on their meaning in light of your relationships. When you are upset with your partner or friend, ask yourself, "At whom am I really upset?" When you determine to give yourself and others compassion, you also ignite the power of passion in your life.

Willingness

Willingness

PRESENT CHALLENGE
Finding value from spending quality time with others even when no change or response is apparent.

You have drawn this card to offer insight into ways to create spiritual community with others. You will benefit from rethinking your expectations for the interactions you have with others, accepting that you can truly be responsible only for your own intentions and actions.

You may feel as if you've stood on the sidelines, wanting to help others or encourage the healing of humanity and/or the planet but unable to find the means to help. Or you may question the effectiveness of the ways in which you have tried to help. You may feel burned out and despairing, or you may feel hopeful yet unsure of the best way to proceed. This card is suggesting that your spiritual work will blossom and that you will be helping in ever greater ways to create global community.

ANGELIC MESSAGE
Willingness

You come into this world fully prepared to participate in community, and so how is it that you often find this participation so difficult? Community, although natural on the spiritual level, is a learned behavior on the personality and ego levels. This suggests that to participate with others in meaningful and enduring relationships, you can benefit from tapping your more natural and basic spiritual essence.

The living elements of the natural world don't struggle to live together, although there is struggle in the nature of their existence. Likewise, you can accept a fresh relationship with all other living things through willingness to observe and live your purpose and allowing others to do the same without judgement or condemnation. You and others are drawn together for a purpose, and part of your involvement with others is also to define a group purpose.

Non-verbal communication is the language of the universe. It is shared by all manner of living things. All life is subject to the influences of ever-expanding circles of energy, beginning with the individual aspects of life and expanding past the physical Earth and on into the physical universe and then the nonphysical worlds. Perception is the language of community, and even though a flower has no external language, no audible voice, it accomplishes its growth with its own kind through a mutually-understood language of perception. Your willingness to accept nature in all of her paradox and inscrutability opens your inner channels to perception and shows you the spiritual essence and nature of other living things, even when you are unable to explain your impressions rationally.

You likewise reach into the hearts of other people most directly not through directives or spoken words but through time you and they spend together with the intention of learning from each other even when no words are spoken. You live with all other living things in community in order to become a witness to the passing of life and to the awakening of the spirit within yourself and others. Perception is learned from a willing heart, which openly accepts the holiness that is present and is desirous of being expressed in all people and living things.

SPIRITUAL OPPORTUNITY

The guidance coming to you through the blue-violet flower image on this card imparts to you the necessity for quiet inner reflection on the nature of your own life and expectations for community. Also implicit in this guidance is that you are destined to help create meaningful interactions, and so you are in need of expanding and improving the perceptual skills you possess, which allow you to read others' intentions and their unspoken words.

Perception is different from intuition because it arises from the spirit rather than the intellect. Intuition expands thinking, feeling, and reasoning but stays within the confinement of what you've already learned. Perception moves outside the knowledge you've gained from past rational experiences and draws on the wisdom of the superconscious of the God-awareness experiences.

APPLICATION

Look around you and ask yourself what perceptions you can glean from the person, plant, rock, cloud, tree, or flower you may see. Imagine that in response to a question or inquiry you might make of a flower, you fashion a blank circle in your mind's eye. Now allow that empty circle to become filled with the "conversation" from the other living thing that you've invited to participate with you. Through this exercise you are trying to acknowledge that all living things sense life in some way and that all living things are aspects of the Divine and have a required role to play on Earth. Your perception can help you understand the way in which they are each important.

Forgiveness

12

Forgiveness

PRESENT CHALLENGE
Accepting responsibility for your life; releasing blame and the judgement of others.

You have drawn this card because immense beauty and opportunity live beneath your old emotional scars. You have reached a point in your life when you are being directed to free up the energy you've tied to old feelings and failures. Even though you may have worked on your dysfunctional patterns for years, this time in your life represents the final pass-through for many of these persisting lessons.

Forgiveness is the basis for spiritual work because it asserts that you can truly know and appreciate only your own life's journey and perspective. Forgiveness comes through turning your attention inward and using the spiritual energy of love to assess your own relationships.

ANGELIC MESSAGE
Forgiveness

Forgiveness is a spiritual initiative rather than one grounded in the emotions or the intellect. It is difficult to forgive others completely without reserving that small corner of your heart that asserts you were right and they were wrong. That is because you may be seeking to forgive others by using a rational explanation for the reason you should forgive. Truly releasing lingering remorse, guilt, or anger through reasoning is impossible. But, once you realize that your failure to forgive hinders the flow of love into your life and the circulation of this essential energy throughout your body and mind, you are capable of forgiving others from a place deep within you.

Love is the nature of the spiritual energy that guides your life and quite literally accounts for the inner balance that maintains physical health and emotional well-being. Forgiving others allows you to release the energy of love into your daily living. The love you need today in your life to help you meet challenges and to maintain your own inner "light" may still be tied to old, unresolved hurts. Any apathy you are experiencing, any confusion, lack of direction, exhaustion, or sense of being overwhelmed, may well stem from captive energy held in the small corners of your heart.

Love is the emotional and spiritual energy that ties you to those who have hurt you. The issues that seem to defy forgiveness are always aligned in some way with love: the love you never received, the love that you offered and others rejected or betrayed, the love that was used to manipulate or control you. Love is the basis of your life's well-being, but in tying your spiritual energy reserves to old hurts you are severely limiting the energy of love available to you in the present moment. Perhaps this is the time to search your heart for those you still need to forgive more fully.

SPIRITUAL OPPORTUNITY

The simplicity and elegance of the single purple flower image on this card shows you quite strikingly your guidance for this day. You have drawn this card of Partnership and relationship in order to expand your current level of spiritual awareness and the love in your life. You are encouraged to release old grievances and reorder each day so that you are no longer accumulating new grievances against yourself or others.

This flower image grows straight and true to its purpose.

You, too, also are emerging from times of less clarity into a more direct and fulfilling life path. This image is not shadowed in any way by yesterday's burdens or troubles, and so you are also encouraged to accept each new day without the carryover of previous troubles, burdens, and grievances. Each evening and each morning you can move through, meditate through, and pray through previous hurts and burdens.

APPLICATION

Energy follows every conversation and interaction. Ask yourself, "Is this exchange with my partner, friend, or child productive? Am I learning, sharing, accepting, participating, or feeling otherwise positively engaged? Have I, or are they, closed down, and are we only going through the motions of sharing?" Experience your different responses to people and situations. Try saying to yourself, "I forgive you, and I forgive me for being caught in the process of change and for our being unable to see each other clearly."

Pay attention to the thoughts you have as you fall asleep and those that are on your mind when you wake up. These thoughts embody the situations and the people needing your forgiveness. Releasing yourself from having to be what others want or need lets you find your own true self. Be true to yourself today by forgiving everyone and everything that you meet. Then you will be free to live in love.

Vulnerability

13

Vulnerability

PRESENT CHALLENGE
Transforming relationships into mutually beneficial and spiritually supportive exchanges.

You have drawn this card because it is time for you to take back your power, to pay attention to the timing of certain important events, and to recognize that you are approaching major decisions that will affect all your key relationships.

You may be emerging from a stressful period, or you may still be in such a period at this time, but the lesson for you is to accept the more impersonal and authentic means of assessing your relationships from your inner wise voice. You have been gaining in your ability to hear and appreciate your own wisdom, and this card comes to you to encourage you to honor this guidance and to re-evaluate all relationships that are based on mutual lack, pain, fear, or poverty of spirit.

ANGELIC MESSAGE
Vulnerability

Vulnerability isn't weakness; it is spiritual strength. Your capacity to be vulnerable grows in direct proportion to your state of genuine wisdom, which acknowledges the transitional nature of physical reality and the enduring quality of the spiritual realm. Vulnerability grows as the need for personal material gain and glory diminishes. As your ego gives way to your authentic spiritual power and presence, you gain true vulnerability, and compassion emerges.

The gateway to becoming vulnerable, open, and clear about your intentions and motivations is the voice of your inner spirit, your wise counsel. When you accept your own human frailties, not as an excuse for inflicting pain or for living with indifference but as a means of increasing your capacity to feel compassion easily, then you are living honestly, and you are becoming vulnerable.

Vulnerability is the natural state of open acceptance and self-responsibility resulting from being in touch with your own awakened spirit. All elements of life, physical or nonphysical, that also live in some way with an awakened spirit will know your true self. You are an open book, capable of being easily read by any living thing that lives by spiritual integrity. And thus we, your angelic teachers, can see you totally, can see all the aspects of your life, no matter that you think you hide behind a physical body or elaborate mental explanations. We see and accept your challenges and encourage your search for your wise voice. We do this without judgement and with the expectation that you will be successful as your capacity for love increases.

SPIRITUAL OPPORTUNITY

The guidance available to you through this card asks you to assess the totality of your relationship(s) from a spiritual, wise-mind perspective rather than only from the part of you that has been wounded or feels a sense of lack.

Symbolically, this flower image shows you the contrast between its golden center core, similar to your spirit, and its dark, sharp, and potentially threatening spears, which represent the inevitable duality and conflict in relationships. This guidance asks you to assess the core nature of your relationship(s) from your own wisdom mind in order to make the most productive decisions.

What were the circumstances and issues that brought you together with your friend or partner? If your relationship(s) has been built on the support of each other around mutual wounds, then this basis for support will need to be shifted to one that involves sharing around mutual abundance and personal power. You may be worried about attracting or actually beginning another relationship that might hold the same old patterns and struggles. Selecting this card suggests that you will be successful in attracting and/or creating a strong and mutually supportive spiritual relationship(s), or in having the courage to leave relationships that are unable to change from a negative and "lack" emphasis to an empowered and spiritually vulnerable one.

APPLICATION

Choose the relationship in your life that is both important to you and in need of change. Explore this relationship without making assumptions of what can be changed and what is immovable. All things are possible when supported by spiritual energy.

Hidden agreements show up when one person seeks to step out of character and act or assert himself or herself in new ways. This behavior is often perceived by the other person as threatening. Try to observe these shifts in emphasis, and agree to have special times each week to explore these shifts, either perceived or actual. Meaningful dialogue is essential in relationships, and if one person is unable or unwilling to participate, then circumstances will either move the person into situations that crack the old veneer or dissolve the relationship(s).

Ask each other what needs are not being met when either of you changes the way you've always acted. Try playing different roles in your relationship, with one person assuming a more assertive role and the other a more submissive one. What do you discover when you assume the role the other plays? Can you accept that you are responsible only for your own change and are able to support the other's opportunity to change as well?

Inner Authority

14

Inner Authority

PRESENT CHALLENGE
Gaining confidence in using your inner wisdom to
sustain relationships.

By drawing this card of Partnership you are being urged to reconsider your opinion of yourself. In appreciating your own inner beauty and inestimable value you become better able to support and interact with the diverse opinions and attitudes expressed by others.

You may be feeling that others often disregard you, fail to meet your needs, or override or undervalue you and/or your efforts. You may feel sometimes overshadowed by others who have more inner authority. You long to be fully united with your own true nature, to eliminate the inner hollowness and find renewed deep health and purpose. This card comes to you in order to encourage you to nurture your inner authority so that you are better able to move into meaningful and fulfilling relationships.

ANGELIC MESSAGE
Inner Authority

Inner authority is spiritual energy born from union with the Divine. Inner authority is seen in what you say and what you don't

97

say, in the quality, tone, and reverence with which you approach all living things. When you speak out of love, out of commitment, out of determination, you are ordering the forces of energy within you and the Universe toward a harmony of purpose, an explosion of power. This inner combustion takes place when you turn your attention inward and give time to your spirit.

You do not need to ask permission to love yourself, because loving yourself is the natural state of humanness. You are encouraged by the Universe to find and live the fullest expression of your own unique nature; nothing less is sufficient to you or God. Your inner authority develops as your need for outer authority diminishes and as you listen continually for the voice of your inner mind, your spirit.

Possessing inner authority is at the core of creating and sustaining lasting relationships and spiritual community. True community is based on each person's willingness and ability to maximize each opening to spiritual growth while also honoring this process in others. People have an underdeveloped inner authority from a lack of commitment to the purpose of their own life, which is to give rise to their spirit's fullest bloom.

Inner authority comes not from immediate material or spiritual "success" but from perseverance. You gain inner authority with the belief and inner expectation that you do have an essential inner beauty that is priceless, worth struggling to uncover and to know. You've come into this life having already lived and blossomed before in many extraordinary ways. Your search now is to uncover this lifetime's essential core so that you may also indirectly absorb the learning from past lives. Your journey is the awakening of your inner authority, and this voice, this spiritual energy, can contribute to your fulfillment in relationships and act as the force to bring you and your Earth into peaceful times.

SPIRITUAL OPPORTUNITY

The guidance available to you through the flower image on this card is to take a long, hard look at the future you hope to create and to realize that it will never be simpler or more difficult than in this moment. The multiple colors, shapes, and designs within this flower show you, symbolically, that your life is never all good or all bad but is rather a continual blend of emotional and spiritual experiences and energies. Your life is never totally clear of obstructions or factors that need resolution. The challenge is to begin to create, one moment at a time, knowing that today, like tomorrow, will have its conflicts.

Your guidance suggests that you can step up to today's opportunities because you have the seeds of spiritual love and awareness already in your life, now within this magnificent blend of sorrow, joy, loss, and gratitude. In placing more emphasis on exploring your own inner authority, you'll be less easily sidetracked or put off by the demands and expectations of others and more able to create the future you choose.

APPLICATION

Write down what your inner authority spiritual voice "sounds" like to you. Observe the people and circumstances in which you already use your inner authority. How does it feel when you use this more aligned inner energy? Why don't you use it with certain others? What do you need in order to use this inner authority voice more often?

Ask those you live with or your closest family members or friends to discuss the idea of an inner authority voice. Ask each person to share with you information about the times and the ways they are able to use their own inner authority voice. Ask each person how each can help the others call forth their own inner voices more often. Place a small sticker on your daily calendar identifying the days in which you feel you are actively using your inner authority and thereby reinforcing this new alignment.

Self-Worth

15

Self-Worth

PRESENT CHALLENGE
Ability to hold your inner balance and to respond to others from your own self-worth.

You have drawn this card to help you recognize the times and the ways in which you give away your inner power. This card suggests that you need to strengthen your feelings of inner confidence and self-worth so that others are not so easily able to break down or deflate your sense of well-being.

You are entering, or may already have entered, a series of experiences to help you test your own ability to hold or reclaim your power. This card is suggesting that you will do well to make sure you stay in your own power even when others have expectations of your fixing their lives.

ANGELIC MESSAGE
Self-Worth

Self-worth is the basis for spiritual advancement. When you accept your own natural capacity for love, compassion, and gratitude, you also unknowingly accept the same qualities in God. You are a mirror reflection of the divine Presence.

You may recognize that you often feel lost or deeply lonely whether or not you are in a relationship or even when you are with other friends. You are feeling the pull of your spiritual roots, of us, your angelic teachers. We were with you before you were born and will again be with you when you leave life. We wish to remind you that your loneliness is your spirit's desire to grow in its capacity to know the sacred Presence. The Divine holds the ultimate capacity to preserve and increase love and self-worth in your life, and it is through this expanding capacity to know God that you come to know yourself.

Your search for self-worth is also humanity's search. As you are propelled through circumstances to help you claim your own goodness and ability to further goodness on the Earth, you move slowly toward the awareness that your life and your talents are best used in service to others. You and the Creator form a bond, and this bond is recognized by you as the means of loving yourself and honoring your own unique qualities.

When you feel alone and disconnected from your inner goodness and perhaps your inner assurance of a caring God, look up into the sky, or over to the mountains, or at the blossoming flowers in your garden. Assure yourself that you are not alone and that all of Nature seeks to find love. There is no need to struggle with life, only to begin to know your own value as a reflection of the sacred in all life.

SPIRITUAL OPPORTUNITY

The guidance coming to you through this flower image shows you most dramatically the contrast between the inner and the outer, between the beliefs you hold and those that are universally inspired that determine the ease with which you accept your life and are able to transcend physical difficulties.

Because self-worth is a steppingstone to self-love, you can continue to create your life in the image of love so that it reflects a deepening capacity to hold love for yourself, for other living things, and for the divine Presence. Relax your fears and spread your goodness for all to see. Explore what you believe. Look and listen to the inner vocabulary you use with yourself and others. If you want to change an external part of your life, then you are first required to change the internal beliefs that hold these patterns in place. If you want others to respond to you or your work in different ways and with more appreciation, then examine your expectations for your work and your efforts. When you believe in yourself, chances are others will find your worth also.

You are becoming more capable of holding your own value while at the same time encouraging others. You may have felt competitive or jealous of others in the past, but you are increasingly striving to accept that your life has ample opportunities for success. You are responsible primarily for developing your own spiritual capacity, and yet along the way you have ample opportunity to help others who are also shifting their perspective to awaken their own self-worth.

APPLICATION

Use your spiritual beliefs and the tools of understanding that accompany these beliefs in your everyday life. Try this energy exercise in any circumstance in which you find it difficult to express your true feelings adequately or to capture the attention of others long enough to convey your meaning. Imagine a broad white band of energy surrounding you and the others in your gathering. In doing this you are drawing forth from each person their truest wisdom and intention. You are also maximizing each person's ability to absorb what is truly meant rather than what was only spoken. This exercise works in extraordinary ways with any number of people: you'll observe in the dynamics of the group that each person exhibits a greater sense of honesty, vulnerability, and sensitivity.

Balance

16

Balance

PRESENT CHALLENGE
Living in the moment and allowing the future to unfold naturally from your own wisdom.

You've drawn this card so that you will be encouraged to take heart that you have entered a time to make new choices and that these decisions are to set the course for future stability in relationships and in life work.

The choices you make each moment are best made when they arise from your own inner wisdom. Only your inner awareness holds the power to direct your life and overcome persistent feelings of lack or failure. By drawing this card you're being notified that, even though you may want others to verify that you are doing the right things, you already have the answers to your most pressing questions. You are in the process of filling any and all inappropriate emptiness with blessings.

ANGELIC MESSAGE
Balance

Living in the moment is one of the most significant universal teachings for improving the quality of your life. Your future takes place in the moment, growing organically from the wisdom you can already lay claim to. Focusing on the wisdom you already know and can apply to your life allows you to remain whole and to avoid being swallowed by pain, confusion, or lack of belief in your own vision. Your own wisdom allows you to observe people and circumstances moving into and out of your life even when you exert mental effort to produce a different outcome.

It is of course much easier to scan the external horizons of your life looking for solutions than it is to grasp the joy you already feel today and to recognize it as your own guidance. There are no paths that lead to certain material success because the material side of creation is based entirely on intentionality. What you believe that is drawn from your spirit is expansive and all-encompassing; it can thus help you create in many ways simultaneously.

Inner balance, unlike physical balance, refers to the process of maintaining inner well-being. When you are balanced you accept and learn from the contrasts in your life more easily because you have an inner presence that holds you together. This reserve is the amassed spiritual energy that comes from monitoring your physical life through a spiritual lens. Your present state of awareness is trying to suggest that there is a difference between mental preoccupation with your life and its goals and the ability to accept the guidance of the emerging "light" within you.

SPIRITUAL OPPORTUNITY

The guidance coming to you through this card is showing you that you need to be more trusting of your own instincts. Red is the color of passion, strong intention, and self-belief. This flower image suggests that many positive new initiatives will find completion or that new creative expressions will take root in your life. Fresh insight and positive occurrences flow from inner balance, and by allowing your wisdom to open to the observance of divine love in your life, you are able to more readily accept an expansion of your accomplishments and success. While your focus may be on a specific person and situation that needs attention at this time, keep from becoming totally preoccupied with this one circumstance, because it may be limiting your spiritual unfoldment. Relax your own expectations, and accept the Universe's initiatives to help you in all ways.

Step outside your daily routine and watch yourself go about your daily living. Do you look tired, stressed out, weary of life and its loads? Do you look refreshed, joyful, playful, filled with good humor and compassion? The difference lies not in your physical circumstances but in the off-setting power and joy of your daily spiritual practices—and these include every aspect of daily life. You have entered a time when you need to deepen and re-establish your internal balance and recognize that it is held in place by your spirit's guidance.

APPLICATION

Physical movement is an essential aspect of maintaining both physical well-being and spiritual balance. Even if you do aerobic exercise, consider also taking time for activities like contemporary dance, T'ai chi, or yoga that help you listen to your internal senses and silences. Or go for a walk, and walk briskly. After several moments, observe the colors that you can see in your inner mind's eye; these are the colors that reflect your mood. If you're feeling in a listening mode, you'll see colors in the pastel hues. If you are in the asserting and acting mode, the colors will be brighter and more dramatic. Ask yourself what question you most need answered, and then allow the world around you to speak to you so that the next step, the immediate goal or answer, can be clearly acknowledged. Try praying while you walk, "Allow me to see clearly the answer, solution, or guidance that I need so that I no longer need to worry that I'm doing the wrong thing."

Power

17

17

Power

PRESENT CHALLENGE
Accepting your capacity for spiritual leadership by expanding your willingness to love.

You have drawn this card to rediscover a deeper capacity for love and compassion. Through implementation of this realization, you will advance into authentic spiritual leadership. You have sought guidance for your own life, and now you are to learn to seek guidance for the lives of others and for the Earth

You are reawakening to your spirit's purpose. You are being guided to accept love without judgement and to use compassion freely, and in so doing to remove any constraints and beliefs you've placed on the power of love to heal, help, change, and awaken grace within all living things. You may be wondering whether you are growing spiritually in the most appropriate ways; you've drawn this card to show you that your prayers have been heard.

ANGELIC MESSAGE
Power

Inner power is divine love, and it is a natural expression of your humanness. When you open your mouth to speak, you anticipate

that words will come out and that these words will convey the meaning you intend. When you open your heart to feel love for another person, for animals, or for Nature, you feel expansive, deeply connected to others through unlimited and unconditional love. These deeply personal and profound feelings that come through meditation as well as through intimate and direct experiences of loving your partner, your children or parents, and your friends are the natural state of your humanness and the basis of spiritual leadership.

Inner power is resilient, it is expressed as empathy for other living things, and it comes forth as nonjudgemental grace. Resilience teaches you to observe your life from a different and deeper perspective, thus enabling you to move around the constraints of pain and loss. Empathy teaches you to trust your natural desire to help others and in return to receive love from people, Nature, and God. Living in grace allows you to teach others through the example of your own life and to offer nourishment through awareness of divine love in action in your life and on the Earth.

The spiritual energy of your life is welling up deep inside you from the core of your being and circling your spine to renew your life. You are in the process of managing this intense emerging energy so that you will direct it toward awakening the God within.

You are being guided to accept your larger role in life and to trust that through the grace of your angelic teachers and the Divine you will be able to recognize your opportunities to balance and stabilize your life, the lives of others, and the Earth's living environment.

SPIRITUAL OPPORTUNITY

The guidance awakened by your drawing this card asks you to express spiritual leadership in the ordinary everyday and every-moment occurrences of your life. Notice the golden image of the pistil, the seed bearer, and its three prominent channels of expression. This flower image alerts you to work with the three major channels of spiritual energy in your own life: resilience, empathy, and grace. This flower offers you a symbolic image of profound importance. You are being guided to recognize that you already have a basis of genuine spiritual understanding and that you will grow in power by using your wisdom in your life in a more direct and uncompromising fashion.

Spiritual resilience is the acceptance that all things are not as they seem. You will find renewal for yourself through living empathetically, a kind of living that has as its basis the realization that the energy of divine love lies within every human plan. And grace is the unconditional gift to humanity of the realization that spirit, in all of its forms in all living things, is indestructible and immortal.

APPLICATION

The next time you look into the face of a person, or symbolically into the darkness of an experience or circumstance that is difficult for you to love and/or accept, imagine that you are observing grace emerging in an unrecognized form to teach you of power and love.

Imagine that you have been guided to become a spiritual leader and that you are apprenticed to that purpose from this time forward. If you believed this, in what ways would you see your life differently? Would you take your spiritual practices and the means of living according to these practices a little more seriously? Would you see coincidence as your daily teacher and the search for unconditional love as the unspoken need beneath every argument? Would you acknowledge more readily the bonds that clearly and directly tie you to God and every living thing? Ask yourself these questions in meditation and, without judging the responses, write down what you've discovered.

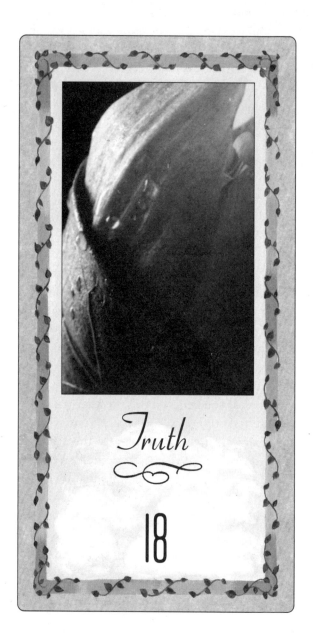

Truth

18

Truth

PRESENT CHALLENGE
Working through denial and accepting the power of your spirit to promote appropriate physical, emotional, or spiritual healing.

Integration cards direct your attention toward inner harmony and balance, and this card seeks to focus your attention on the ways in which you can open yourself to the truth of your situation rather than living in denial.

You have drawn this card to help you find the clarity you need to make important choices for your life. This is a powerful card of healing, and you have drawn it because you are seeking to understand the significance of your present challenges and to clearly determine the course of action that will best support all aspects of your well-being.

ANGELIC MESSAGE
Truth

As inevitably as the moon changes phases or the flowers blossom from their buds, you also are required to seek your own truth. You may think that there is only one truth; yet we, your angels, suggest that all of you have your own truth, your own interpretation of divine law. No one way is right or wrong because all aspects of the

113

divine plan are being birthed on Earth simultaneously. And yet your spirit is asserting that a single truth is emerging for you, and it is seen through the awareness and grace gathered from past experience.

Fear is the only enemy of living in a truthful way. Fear robs you of clarity and peace of mind and substitutes instead a false bravado that holds no power. Are you afraid of the truth? Are you afraid that you will hear from those you love and depend on that you are unworthy, unlovable, or offering little value? Are you afraid to know the diagnosis that may tell you that your time on the Earth is limited? Are you afraid for your children to fail? Are you fearful that you will never find a life worth living? Are you afraid of being alone? Fear is a powerful means of holding you in denial and preventing you from accepting the truth of your present challenge, which is to accept the magnificence of your life with all its struggles as the vehicle through which you are to learn to recognize your own spiritual truth.

Truth is not a death sentence or a pronouncement from on high that is punitive in nature. Rather, truth is the means through which you can honor and evaluate the meaning of your passing physical life. Truth is the acceptance of your spirit's voice and a willingness to work in whatever way is required to honor the day and to honor the Force that brings you life.

SPIRITUAL OPPORTUNITY

The guidance emerging for you through this flower image suggests that this is a time to take stock of your life. This wondrous image of green and orange, healing and balance, expresses the universality and eternal process of life and death, emergence and release. This image is guiding you to become more aware of the deeper spiritual currents in your life, which are directing you toward a new beginning and also toward learning from the experiences and relationships that may be coming to a close.

You are being alerted that your spiritual currents, the ones that teach you of your life mission and your immortality, are more available to you. You are also being shown that you are becoming more sensitive to learning and insight from past lifetimes. This is a most meaningful time of personal spiritual synthesis for your life. Practice taking no action until you are sure that the action you choose flows from your deeper truth and wisdom.

APPLICATION

Think of the greatest challenge to your well-being that you face at this time. Now pretend you can step outside your life, away from having any vested interest in your situation. Try observing your situation with dispassion. Notice how difficult it is to avoid feeling the pull of your emotions as they try to show you the images of your worst fears. But be persistent. First consider the openings and opportunities that are in your life or are coming into it. Now think about the aspects of your life that are closing down or moving away from you, even though you might have it otherwise. Try not to fight what your spirit is suggesting. Joy and well-being always follow your spirit's guidance even if, in the short term, it means that you will have hurdles, even difficult ones, to cross.

Ask your inner truth, the all-knowingness part of you, to stay with you and eliminate or reduce fear. Imagine that you are sitting in the lap or held in the arms of the person or teacher you most love, whether or not this presence is on the Earth. Feel the currents of love as they flow through your body and your emotions. You are safe, and no harm can ever come to you. Relax, breathe, and accept that all is well.

Expression

19

19

Expression

PRESENT CHALLENGE
Unleashing spiritual energy and overcoming limitations.

You have drawn this card of Expression in order to further your personal spiritual growth and to help call to your attention those ways in which you box in and limit your spirit's energy.

Even if you have worked on healing past painful experiences or dysfunctional attitudes, this card is asserting that you can further or even finish this release work by paying particular attention to color and its healing energy. You have drawn this powerful card of self-expression in order to further awaken your spirit's presence and to reorder and deepen your beliefs about God.

ANGELIC MESSAGE
Expression

The search for divine realization is your search and your children's and grandchildren's search, too. You express the magnificence of love only as you experience God's love. You and all living things are the colors of this expression of divine love. You have specific physical characteristics, and these are to honor your own uniqueness as well as the entire divine system of life. The color of your skin, the color of your clothes, your house, your car, and your friends: all are expressions of divine love. God is woven into all life because God is life. You and God share the same bed, the same car, the same glass of water. You and God are one.

Your spirit, as part of this grand divine plan, isn't bound by your physical body's boundaries. In your daily life you are aware that a part of you is tied directly to the physical body through laughter or tears, happiness or fear. These mental expressions of your physical reality change as quickly as your clothes. Your spiritual expression, however, remains constant. It is the guiding light within. Your spirit is urging you continually to live with love and compassion; and beyond your desire to understand God, merely loving your way into the realization of God.

Your spiritual body is in no way limited because your mind is unable to follow into uncharted realms of energy. The next time you are tied up in knots emotionally, try to catch the fleeting impression of your spirit, and you will sense an entirely different energy. The time you feel the least like looking for spiritual insight is often the time you will be the most successful, because spiritual orientation can come through clearly during mental disorientation.

SPIRITUAL OPPORTUNITY

The guidance through this flower image is to be aware that your inner voice can trumpet out into your life and into the world, sharing feelings that grow from an unlimited spiritual reality: truth, love, joy, kindness, compassion, and service. The varying darkness and lightness of the purple flower petals alerts you to the truth that your entire life is a spiritual search. Some days you will feel more directly aligned with the Divine, and on other days you will feel more limited, upset, and distant from God, but the colors of God's love are always available to you.

The divine Presence is never far away, never distant from your problems and concerns. But the divine Presence also doesn't accept problems as the excuse for denying love. The vast and all-encompassing energy of God knows that a different realization is possible for humanity. In order to "see" and "feel" God at work in your life, you need to find and use the gifts of insight and perception available to you.

APPLICATION

To call on the energy of your spirit for healing of yourself or others, close your eyes and imagine that you can perceive a boundary or outline around your physical body. This outline often appears as an oval. Where the physical body is healthy, a blue/purple border is visible around the perimeter of the body. Where illness is present, the border is often broken, missing, or appears to be black or dark grey.

Healing involves understanding the emotions that have broken down your aura of health. In meditation, ask to understand the nature of the force that holds disease, dysfunction, or disturbance in place in your life. Ask yourself what passion may have been thwarted in your life that you desire to recognize and recapture. As you approach the accurate negative feelings or responses, the blue-purple border around your body will begin to reappear. This means healing has begun.

Synchronicity

20

Synchronicity

PRESENT CHALLENGE
Accepting that everything happens for a reason and that each event now occurring in your life has benefits.

You have drawn this card because some striking synchronicities have taken place or are about to take place in your life, and you may be unsure whether to view these events as guidance or merely coincidence.

This is an Integration card and it seeks to encourage you in establishing and maintaining your inner balance. This card brings you assurance that you are linked directly to your angelic teachers and to the God-source through your willingness to accept thoughts, feelings, and events in your life as clear and specific spiritual guidance bent on awakening you fully within this lifetime to the nature of God.

ANGELIC MESSAGE
Synchronicity

What is guidance? When you ask the Universe to be with you and guide your life, do you recognize that this is a living prayer and has profound manifestations on the etheric levels? Prayers—asking for help and a path through anguish and struggle—are met with immediate and direct angelic attention and intervention. When you pray, for example, you may feel better immediately. When you meditate, you may momentarily discover a renewal that you are unable to explain. When you release fear and accept a sequence of events different from those you wanted, you may feel strangely loved and safe. These are all the quiet but certain blessings of grace brought to you by your invocations.

Synchronicity is also the blessings of grace at work in your life, but it suggests that you are preparing to take physical action in some way and that you are being called upon to seek your true motivation and expectations for desired change. Synchronistic events help you appreciate that a deep level of change has been sought and is being addressed, and that it is important for you to understand the spiritual significance of this change rather than merely accepting it on the physical and emotional levels. You are being challenged to act only when you are clear about the spiritual components involved in your leaving, changing, and accepting something tangibly different for your life.

The flower, for example, grows regardless of synchronous events. It lacks the physical choices that human beings enjoy. The flower grows in direct alignment with its purpose as it senses it. People, on the other hand, are always attracting choices. When you can identify your true motivations and needs, then you can reflect on the synchronicities you are drawing to you, and you can benefit from impending physical, emotional, and spiritual shifts meant to further your spiritual awakening.

SPIRITUAL OPPORTUNITY

Your guidance through this flower image is to recognize that everything happens for a reason even though the reason may not be apparent immediately. The green tones of this flower tell you that you've drawn a card of healing, and the sharply contoured petals suggest that some contrasts are about to come into your life or may already have arrived. The fact that the petals are in pairs offers the thought that you'll have at least two major choices around this change, and you most assuredly want to choose the one that will lead to success.

What should you do? What is the right answer for this challenge? Look deeply into this flower image, and you will see the answer. Both petals grow from the center, or spiritual core. Any change point thus always has several solutions, and no one choice is either all right or all wrong.

Synchronicities in your life are meant to alert you that a change is necessary and that you need to activate your inner perceptual skills to create the awareness of the positives and perceived negatives that will result from each choice.

APPLICATION

Some synchronicities are obvious: meeting the same person in unlikely places three times in one week, or having the name of a particular city or state pop up over and over when you are searching for a place to live. Deeper synchronicities are also observable in the way the natural flow of your life works to separate you from people and/or relationships. You overhear a telephone conversation "by chance" or you open a piece of mail that you misread and thought was addressed to you, for example, and discover that people are making choices and are talking about feelings that you were unaware they had.

Spiritual synchronicity occurs when you keep hearing the same inner phrase or thought over and over. In your meditation, you may hear, "Accept your life and the teachings that are coming to you." Driving to work, you may listen to a tape in which the speaker talks about the power of accepting the challenges of your life as your teachers. At lunch, your friend may ask you if you've read a book called *Accepting Life as Your Teacher*. In all these examples of synchronicities, you are being given an inside understanding that change is occurring and that you are to glean all that you can without blame or judgement so that you are free to move on with your life. Even if you don't want to move on, the events in your life show you that a greater purpose is being played out.

Emergence

21

Emergence

PRESENT CHALLENGE
Surrendering to your inner power and overcoming the need to control the outcome of the events in your life.

You have drawn this card because your immediate struggle may deal with the need to release control of your life so that you can deepen your relationship with the guidance from your own spirit and move more fully into the true intention and purpose for which you are living.

This is a card meant to help you understand the difference between surrender and capitulation, between genuine bonding with angelic wisdom and your need to remain separate and alone. You have drawn this card because your life is bent on taking you toward renewed inner power and new levels of joy.

ANGELIC MESSAGE
Emergence

Life is confusing when you listen only to your rational thinking, because your mind knows only rational solutions, and the resolutions you seek grow from spiritual understanding, which is not necessarily arrived at deductively. Your heart, your inner mind or spirit, is the great conveyer of wisdom and truth because it knows what the mind does not; it has lived where the mind has not. When you listen to your heart you are placed in direct alignment with those teachings and teachers who seek to enter your awareness and to whom you may unknowingly have extended an invitation to help you on your spiritual journey.

The way to experience a spiritually awake heart is to move intentionally into your own thinking patterns to sort through your need to maintain control over your life. You are only one step away from our guidance, because we are the angels who help you in small yet essential ways, which include breathing love into your life each second of every day. We ask you to confront your fear of the unknown and to come and participate in the creative, ebullient, and colorful expressions of life we offer to show you.

In order for you to emerge more fully into the experience of spiritual love, we ask you to explore your fear of surrendering to divine love. Capitulation and surrender are two words that are often confused; the first arises from the mind and the second from the spirit. Capitulation is what you may have experienced in the past when you were forced to accept another's opinions and choices for your life. Surrender, by contrast, is the spiritual response to an acceptance and absorption into God's love, truth, and presence. You reach the point of surrender daily in small, seemingly insignificant ways and at major life turning points. The process of surrender, in large or small ways, is the same and offers you the opportunity to accept love and perennial guidance. The emotions awakened through your inner vision are vastly different from mental emotions. They shed light on your past, give hope to your future, and, most important, give impetus to the moment you have in front of you to be lived purposefully.

SPIRITUAL OPPORTUNITY

The guidance to you through this flower image is that emergence of love in your heart is already underway. The soft green buds, still tightly closed at the center of the flower, show you that healing is taking place right now in your life. The pink flowers opening to the light signify the loving kindness you are learning to use with those you love and those you struggle to love.

The beauty and emergence of the buds and blossoms of this flower depict both the possibilities for your life and the traps that your rational mind would have you accept as genuine limitations. This image suggests that you are in the right place for spiritual emergence even if you have problems remaining unsolved and questions remaining unanswered. Accept that you are being guided by the angels, that you are in the stream of divine Love, and that you are healing the old pains, fears, and confusions that have caused you to try to control your destiny mentally. You need to accept that you are part of a larger plan and that each day you will discover more of the part you play in it.

APPLICATION

Your concerns are part of the natural human search for God and the personal realization that no separation lies between you and the Universe. All opportunities are open to you as you seek love. When things take shape in ways other than you had planned, do you feel ignored or overlooked by the Universe and/or your teachers? Are you frustrated that you've been unable to develop a more specific relationship with your angelic guides? Do you try to sort out your life's problems all by yourself? Are you plagued with periods of disbelief that stem from wondering whether your teachers and guides are really what you've come to believe they are?

To reinforce your beliefs, meditate upon this thought: imagine that you are shining your inner light out into the world, out through any and all mental resistance that you put up to protect yourself. Imagine that this inner light has immense power, and when you shine it out through the fog of your disbelief, concern, or fear, it inevitably finds and merges with divine consciousness. And in this way you find belief in your own spiritual emergence.

Purpose

22

Purpose

PRESENT CHALLENGE
Discovering your means of service and living it unconditionally.

You've drawn this Alignment card to help you understand the nature of your life work and to accept that right now you are living some version of your mission.

This card's guidance to you involves accepting that your meaningful work is unfolding as you awaken spiritually and that the process can be speeded up only through personal spiritual practice. In seeking your life's means of service and contribution to humanity, you may eventually need further schooling, or you may need to move or change in external ways, but these opportunities will flow smoothly into your life as the natural extension of your inner joy.

ANGELIC MESSAGE
Purpose

Because of the culture in which you live, you are conditioned to pick a trade or job, to choose a partner, and to determine the part of the country and the sort of housing in which you will live. And now you search for more specific guidance as to the means of using your abilities to help and heal humanity and the Earth.

129

In the largest sense, of course, your daily living is your spiritual work. But we, your angels, know you want to find or deepen your specific means of service. How, then, do you find the specific ways to accomplish these things that you came to the Earth to do if it is impossible to choose them with your mind? The answer is that you choose them with your heart, and then your mind can put its efforts into giving form and presence to this inner awareness.

Let us imagine a hypothetical meditation in which you ask the Universe to show you the way to find and live your means of service. You say, "Please show me the means of finding what I'm to do with my life."

We say, "Dear one, you are already doing your work. Look more closely at those you love and help each day. Observe the people to whom you are an inspiration, those you encourage or have enlightened in some way. Watch the joy you feel in some of the specific work you do today and draw closer to it because it is the jewel of your life; it is your service."

You say, "Yes, but I want to know now what to do. I'm tired of searching and waiting, and I have bills to pay. I'm ready to put my talents to work for the Universe," you insist.

And we say, "Trust, relax, pay attention to the voice of your spirit, and follow it into your joy—this is your work. Press onward into this essence of joy, do those things without pay, without regard for praise, recognition, or even encouragement, and acts quietly and humbly performed will turn into the job that pays you or the means of doing and accomplishing the work that needs doing in ways supported by the physical world."

We say, "Keep your joy foremost in your mind and resist the seduction of your ego, which needs to give your service instant shape. Begin in small and simple ways with the means that are already in your life. People and Nature have needs that you can fill right now. Push away the demands of your ego, and listen attentively to the joy radiating from your soul."

Perhaps something in our words will strike a chord that helps you accept the love and life that is already yours. Your life and your personal spiritual evolution are both in progress, always in the process of discovery. It is your choice whether to remove your gaze *from the mountaintop long enough to discover the reality of the ground at your feet.*

SPIRITUAL OPPORTUNITY

The guidance available to you through this card is seen in the sharp contrast between the creamy pink flower petals and the stark black background. You have drawn this card to help you realize that you are well served to focus on your inner nature before checking the want ads. Observe your natural predisposition toward certain kinds of people, activities, and interactions. What you do willingly and effortlessly opens your heart to love and leads to the enhancement of your own goodness and self-worth, thus manifesting into the tangible means of service you seek or desire to deepen.

APPLICATION

Think of a recent experience in which you said or did something you liked and felt good about, an experience in which you helped in some way. How did you feel during and after the experience? Write down this experience, and then summarize your feelings about your effectiveness in one or two sentences beginning with "I." This will give you a clear sense of your own goodness. You might write, for instance, "I am able to instill a sense of peace in people when they are very upset," or, "I am able to synthesize complex situations and explain them so others can easily understand and be reassured," or "I can handle animals with respect, and they understand and are helped by my presence and work."

As you recognize your goodness, then you recognize the ways in which you already use it. This means you are already living your purpose. Your purpose is first "to be" and then "to do."

Release

23

23

Release

PRESENT CHALLENGE
Relinquishing struggle and accepting the truth of your angelically-inspired perception.

You have drawn this card to help you validate your inner feelings about the work you are already doing, want to do, or dream about creating that is your gift to humanity and the planet.

This is a critical card of Alignment because it calls you to accept your own guidance and a spiritual perspective to your life. This card is also calling you to recognize that you may be sinking or stuck in the quicksand of your rational dialogue, and it is your cue to move into the perspective of your divine nature. You are being asked to see the value in your life as, without hesitation, you give love, appreciation, and compassion to yourself and others.

ANGELIC MESSAGE
Release

Do the angelic kingdoms truly influence your life? Can you reduce pain and recycle self-destructive feelings and attitudes into compassionate and self-accepting ones? The answer is unequivocally "yes," although it takes consistent desire and attention to bring about long-standing change. Your spirit seeks to draw you into an awakened state, because this is all that it knows. When you meditate, pray, and try to live in awareness of your divine nature and the divinity of all other things, then you awaken grace and reduce struggle, no matter the physical circumstances you find yourself in.

Your awakened spirit is the bud of love and God-realization in your life. Consider the flower bud as it seeks the light of its purpose. You might wonder why it does not get confused and disoriented in making its way into life. You might imagine correctly that it has no other choice, and its life is pre-ordered to only accept its purpose. You are pre-ordered in basically the same way, because you and the flower both search for the physical and spiritual light.

Struggle is part of living on Planet Earth. Mental struggle is mitigated by spiritual awareness. When you find even momentary peace of mind it is because you have called on your ability to accept and give love and compassion. You will have accepted that you have a Buddha nature, a wisdom mind that can merge with the awareness from other teachers, avatars, and masters to bring you into alignment with your highest self. It is only in this state of highest self that you can glimpse joy and release pain and the fear of abandonment and death.

Consider this card as affirmation of your immediate ability to claim your highest self and release the needy aspects of your life that mentally hold you prisoner. As you find ways to relax your mind and find your spirit, the perceived limitations of your mental view will slowly vanish. Accept your own wisdom mind and those impulses that flow to your spirit from God, impulses that you can discover through your deep intuition. Here for your use in meditation is a powerful mantra that will encourage the process of release and acceptance of the true nature of your divinity:

"I am love, I give love, I accept love, I believe in love, I extend love, I am always becoming love."

SPIRITUAL OPPORTUNITY

The guidance coming to you through this flower image helps you accept that you may find a diversity of authentic approaches to spiritual study and growth. Notice the brilliance of the healing green color as the buds gradually open to more subtle hues. These buds are symbolically your own spiritual impressions and feelings emerging from a wide variety of sources. Reading good spiritual literature, for instance, does much to awaken your own perceptions of what has merit and appeal to you. When you first hear of specific spiritual insights, interpretations, or observations, you may not accept some of them, or even any of them, as relevant for your path. If you've been raised in a particular religion, you may be tempted to feel that only one way is the authentic path to God.

Your guidance through this card is to keep an open mind, to observe all that crosses your path, and to sense from your heart whether what you are reading or listening to has validity. Wherever it is genuine, your own perception will lead you toward love, compassion, and self-understanding.

APPLICATION

This card is drawing your attention to your need to believe more in yourself and in your divine guidance.

When you feel discouraged, try releasing all the mental busy-ness by fixing your attention on one solid object or beautiful image. Hold your attention here until the mental struggle abates and you find a sense of renewal emerging within your heart. This is a simple means of reaffirming the presence of your awakened spirit and its alignment with everything else in the Universe. Try writing out an affirming statement of your acceptance of guidance in your life and placing it next to or underneath this card. An example of such a statement would be, "I acknowledge my divine self and ask to live with awareness of this sublime love."

Trust

24

24

Trust

PRESENT CHALLENGE
Acknowledging universal love as your basis for bonding with others.

You have drawn this card to reinforce your belief in a loving Universe and to awaken new channels through which you can use the Universe's love to strengthen your ties with other people, with animals and other living things, and with the work that you offer as service to humanity and the planet.

You may be experiencing, or are about to experience, an accelerated period of spiritual growth and breakthrough in which your definition of love will change. Still, you are encouraged to maintain your trust and belief in yourself as a worthy and effective vehicle of positive action. Whatever your fears, whatever your insecurities, the angels are working with you to bring you into greater clarity with the nature of love.

ANGELIC MESSAGE
Trust

You are learning to love, and this is for sure. You are also in need of deepening your capacity to love, and to do this you are, with each meditation and act of service, expanding your soul, which is the symbolic chalice into which the energy of love, your spirit, flows. Love as we, your angelic teachers, speak of it, is "the capacity to allow all other living things to grow into their fullest expression of self." The love that you are learning to give is the same that you long to receive: without judgement, accepting of differences, kind and forgiving, hopeful and courageous. This is the love that we offer to you and all of humanity and that we encourage you to seek and use in all ways throughout your life.

Trust holds love in place in your life. Trust grew initially through your loving relationship with God. Then, as you came into physical existence, you decided whether or not you could trust your parents, family, and peers. In all likelihood you've trusted those who you've felt let you down or hurt you, even substantially and without seeming provocation. You may have withdrawn your love from others as a result of rejection or abuse, and today you may be tempted to hold love in abeyance, afraid that others will again break the bonds of trust that you've established.

Love is a renewable energy because it flows from God. Trust, on the other hand, is humanly designed and serves to bond people to God, people to each other, and people to all life on the Earth. While trust can be broken, it can always be re-created because the love upon which it is based is always forthcoming, if not from people then from God. Trust begins from one source and permeates its environment. And so as you live in alignment with the loving universe, you offer to others the ability to change and heal by building bridges of trust that cross the gulfs of human pain.

SPIRITUAL OPPORTUNITY

The guidance coming to you through the delicate image on this card is one of inner tenacity and outward beauty and creativity. You are being guided to see that you can trust others more as you trust that you are living up to the value and worth that the Universe places on you. Your own intuition about other people and circumstances is symbolically as brilliant and clear as the center of this flower. Trust that you are loved and held in tender regard by your angels and by God.

The deep, velvety darkness around this flower image also has a message for you: "Transformation of your old ways of thinking are underway, and you are emerging into kindness." Peers will begin to look to you for your guidance and insight while others may feel jealous or threatened by your self-assurance and clarity. Maintain your own balance, and focus on spiritual solutions to every difficulty. Give freely, because you understand the nature of change, and you know that love is always emerging even around the edges of pain or sadness. God is always present.

APPLICATION

Begin your daily meditation each morning by choosing a question or issue that needs attention in your life. Then, after your morning quiet time, go outside and choose a flower, buy a flower, or select a house plant that seems to call you. If you are going to pick a flower, be sure to thank it for growing and ask it to withdraw its life force energy before it is picked. Place the flower in some obvious spot so that your attention will fall on it often throughout the day. At the end of the day, spend a few minutes alone with the flower and see if you can put into concrete words what your angelic messengers have been saying to you all day. This is a valuable exercise when you need a lot of help and guidance to move through a difficult or painful situation and to reassure yourself that you are making the right choices for your life.

Challenge

⌒∽◦∽⌒

25

25

Challenge

PRESENT CHALLENGE
Accepting spiritual initiation as the birthing of your dreams.

You have drawn this card because you are undergoing a period of spiritual initiation in order to give a specific presence and form to your dreams, hopes, and expectations.

The guidance from this card suggests that you are being called to finish up old business, both physical and spiritual, in order to move forward with your life physically and spiritually. You are also being guided to relax and accept the guidance that is coming to you from your angelic teachers rather than feeling you must do everything for yourself and by yourself. This card deals specifically with the fulfillment of certain specific dreams and/or aspirations that you've felt were to be part of your life, offering your personal skill and spiritual insight to be of service to humanity.

ANGELIC MESSAGE
Challenge

The true challenge in your life involves your willingness to confront your own inner demons and to allow your deeply-felt dreams and aspirations from your spirit to surface into your life. This is called initiation.

Many cultures initiate their own spiritual students, and we, your angelic teachers, also initiate our own. Initiation requires you to release preconceived ideas about the period of training you are entering and to accept the higher good and spiritual guidance that places you under the protection and inspiration of the Universe.

This is a time when looking around and assessing your life on the basis of what you've already accomplished would be foolhardy, because you've accomplished little compared to what you may accomplish in your lifetime. Initiation is part of a sacred ritual for those entering an important spiritual passage. And because a spiritual passage may be upon you, you will need to accept a deeper and more profound insight into the nature of your life. A deeper resolve and greater intuitive appreciation of the life you were meant to live is the result of the period you are presently in.

You face the challenge of failing to believe that the change underway in your psyche is of the Universe's doing and not due only to physical or emotional causes. You have not failed, but you are being sought to acknowledge the power of the sacred in your life and on the Earth. You are being asked to trust the Universe because you are awakening to dreams, visions, and spiritual understanding that will serve you well in this life.

Your means of service in your life is being awakened, strengthened, and blessed; and you are being challenged to accept this spiritual initiation because you are an Earth pioneer with important work to do.

SPIRITUAL OPPORTUNITY

The guidance coming to you through this flower image is to trust your dreams and recognize that it is divine love that brings your desires into actuality. The deep red/crimson flower petals show you, symbolically, the intensity and variety of inner dreams and desires that you hold in your heart and ask you to decide which of these may be ready to be shown to others and to be lived openly.

You no longer need to live without, or at the "bottom of

the barrel," seeking only the dregs or leftovers from life. You are made of the essence of perfection, and you are being encouraged to overcome resistance from inside yourself, or from others, and to give your dreams a chance to grow in the world. There is no one single right or wrong way to proceed. All is possible when living within the grace of God.

APPLICATION

Try manifesting your dreams spiritually. Look into your heart and ask yourself, "What dreams do I have? What do I long for or feel compelled to do with my life?" Now draw these dreams out into the light of day as if they had a physical presence and were real "things," because words do have the power to awaken your own inner resources and belief in yourself.

You are challenging whatever inner messages tell you that you cannot, have not, will not. Re-tell yourself daily the dream you want fervently to come true, and use the present tense, such as "I am _____, or "I am choosing to _____." You are being called to accept this period of initiation and are free to consider enterprises previously considered daring or risky. The Universe and your teachers are working with you, and you are under the positive influences of initiation. Run all choices past your deeper intuition rather than your mental programming.

Acknowledgement

26

26

Acknowledgment

PRESENT CHALLENGE
*Accepting your essential self as the key to discovering
or expanding your life mission.*

You have drawn this card to encourage you in your search for a
way to give your life work more specific form and/or to attract
the people and opportunities that are essential for you to expand
and deepen your means of service to humanity and the Earth.

This cards holds the power of your full potential to realize
your heart's desire. By believing in yourself, the Universe, and
your mission, you can move into a period of manifestation of
the specifics you've been searching for: people, job opportunities, and/or financial backing. Even though you may have
reservations about your abilities or are vague about the
specifics of your mission, you are nevertheless being directed
to pursue your purpose actively.

ANGELIC MESSAGE
Acknowledgment

*You are not alone! How often it must seem that you are isolated
from love and from the confidence to know with certainty that you
are living according to the purpose for which you incarnated. The*

struggle, however, is only rational, because many opportunities will come your way in this life, and you will know inside your heart when the right ones are presented to you. Your essential self, your inner wisdom, is the energy that guides you toward and into your purpose. Your ego asserts what you need to do to please others or to fill feelings of lack or failure. We, your angelic teachers, expect nothing of you save that you listen to your heart and accept each day as a call to use compassion in your thinking about yourself and others.

You may often wonder if the chance to join a certain group of people or travel to a specific spiritual place will help you find your work. The more you surround yourself with people who also acknowledge a responsibility to awaken the spiritual impulses on the Earth, the more love and positive energy will surround you. When you listen to your heart and respond from this place to take up certain work, it is more apt to be fulfilling.

In your relationships with others, as you and they seek to live on purpose with the Universe's will, try to be mindful that you and they are being challenged maximally to live above and beyond the pull of your egos. Your friends are also filled with uncertainty and are also seeking the deep conviction that they are doing the Universe's work. Be gentle in your interactions. You are not measuring your value or worth against their accomplishments, for you and they are entirely different. When you want guidance, listen to your heart. Ask and you most surely will be shown many ways you can be useful.

You are being alerted to the opportunities to further your work because your love and determination to be of service are essential to support the Earth in these times of multi-layered change and uncertainty. The Universe assists change as the inevitable and eternal process of living purposefully on the Earth, and you are merging your abilities with your spiritual assurance from us. You are moving into the light of acknowledgement, accepting that you are held eternally in divine love.

SPIRITUAL OPPORTUNITY

The guidance to you through this flower image is suggesting that you more readily accept your own perceptions and guidance as the basis for expanding your life work and/or service. The brilliant yellow flowers have a radiance that comes through them rather than entirely of them. Your life is similarly brilliant because of the loving energy that comes from the Universe through you and into the world.

Yellow is the color of the intellect, and the guidance from this card is offering that you may be too easily seduced by the apparent "rightness" of rational choices. You may therefore be missing the benefits from choices made at the perceptual level. You may already have, or are developing, a healthy respect for the necessity of a balance between your mind's activities and your heart's perceptions. This card is guiding you to realize that while this balance is important, you are well served to allow your spirit to initiate your plans or directives although permitting your mind to implement them.

APPLICATION

Remind yourself that when you arise in the morning and smile at the day, you are acknowledging your purpose. When you make breakfast and pet the cat, you are acknowledging your purpose. When you get into your car and drive to work you are able to also move in alignment with your inner impulses, your essential self. When you feel frustrated, angry, upset, diminished, or in any way out of balance, it isn't necessarily "the work" that is wrong, only that momentarily you've ceased acknowledging your essential self. Accept that sometimes you will inevitably be pulled away from inner balance, and when this happens, take a breath, look out the window, walk around your office, or smile. In this way your inner nature is again given precedence to lead you fully into your purpose.

Commitment

27

27

Commitment

PRESENT CHALLENGE
*Willingly accepting the spirit of your life purpose even
when it has no physical form.*

You have drawn this card to reaffirm your belief in yourself and
your ability to fulfill your purpose even when your mission
remains at the spiritual level and without obvious physical form.

You are being guided to awaken a more balanced perspective
in your life by expanding your capacity to hold love in your
heart so that other people and living things may heal. You are
being asked to accept that in this lifetime your mission may not
be obvious or take physical form and yet is essential to the evolution of the planet and humanity. You are being alerted to hold
the intentions of love, justice, faith, compassion, and kindness
in your heart so that others may be able to more easily accept
these spiritual qualities into their own lives.

ANGELIC MESSAGE
Commitment

*Because you are physical, and your environment is physical, it
seems realistic to expect that your means of helping and being of
service will also take some physical form. This is not always an*

accurate assessment. Sometimes you incarnate to be specifically of spiritual service alone. If this is true for your life and you've been unable to find an obvious or consistent means of offering your value to others, you may wonder if you're doing something wrong or if you're out of the range of God's love.

You may have chosen in this lifetime to pursue a purely spiritual means of service in order to test your belief in yourself and the Universe, knowing that in this way you were to finally find the true nature of your worth. You may also have chosen this means of intangible spiritual service because you accepted the challenge of holding the presence of love on the Earth so that others could find it more easily. This purpose is that of the ultimate healer. You may be living love quietly, offering love to others, and learning to find and/or accept love in return. In accepting that you are not meant to find one specific tangible means of service at this time, or even for this lifetime, you will be more able to allow your love to flow into many forms that give you pleasure.

If you are a person who has chosen an intangible means of service, then some of the following aspects to your life will have been true. You may have tried many jobs/careers/or challenges, and even though you were good at them you felt as if you were to do something else. You may have experienced a profound sense of love with a specific person in your life, and then that person died, or left, or you became separated from her or him. Your life may not have turned out the way you imagined it would, and yet you have many friends, and people seem to gravitate toward you to tell you their problems and seek counsel. You may often feel lonely spiritually, as if you have a large hole in your heart. You may be deeply affected by the daily news of trauma to animals, children, indigenous people, or others who seem defenseless.

If many of these conditions fit your life, then you can benefit from accepting that you are a teacher of love in this lifetime, you are a holder of the spiritual balance on the Earth so that human evolution can proceed more easily.

SPIRITUAL OPPORTUNITY

The guidance coming to you through this flower is suggesting that your life is a direct reflection of the Divine presence. The gentle purple essence of these blossoms tells you that your life is based on spiritual qualities even if these are not presently in any obvious form. Two flower blossoms are in this image, and they lie directly opposite each other. The flower blossom that is on the bottom symbolically represents you seeking God. The flower blossom on the top represents God and the angelic teachers radiating love to you. The guidance through this card is that you are being asked to commit your full attention toward the living of your spirituality, because this is to be your means of service.

APPLICATION

Try observing the ways in which you do reflect love into people's lives. What have friends or family asked you to help with? In what way are you steadily balancing and encouraging others to honor their true feelings and to be honest with their spiritual path for this lifetime? When you observe yourself living as God's agent of love, you reinforce your worth and importance, committing your life fully to this important work.

Write out your own definition of divine love that is your credo. Create a simple meditation/prayer that you can use to encourage yourself in sharing love with others even when they are unable to thank you or return the favor.

Courage

28

28

Courage

PRESENT CHALLENGE
Persevering even when the work you've begun seems to falter.

You have drawn this card to fortify your resolve and to let you know that you are on the right inner path whether or not the outward signs in your life suggest success.

This is an Alignment card and so is meant to help further focus your attention on your full acceptance of your personal gifts and abilities, the spiritual and physical resources available to you, and your vision that is forever your guide. You may feel that you have been following guidance and now wonder whether you are doing the right thing, because you've met unexpected obstacles. You've drawn this card to learn something new about the spiritual resources available to you.

ANGELIC MESSAGE
Courage

You can count your physical resources more easily than your spiritual ones. Spiritual resources are your ability to find God through peaceful and inspiring meditation, through seeing beauty in those around you and in yourself, and in accepting abundance and joy as your rightful companions in this lifetime. In short, spiritual resources become available to you through the courage to experience life as a living prayer and each moment as an affirmation of the blessings received.

Humanity's challenge has always been, and will continue to be, the search for union with the Divine. While this may sound lofty and difficult, every person eventually seeks inner peace and confirmation of a spiritual dimension no matter the words they choose. It is too difficult to live in Earth School without an awakened spirit. Consider the courage of the flower as it pushes forth its stamen and pistil to reproduce its kind. The flower affirms its beauty and elegance just as you can. You are beautiful and have an elegant spirit when you live in love and use compassion as your aid. And these qualities are everlasting.

When you place your belief in other people and in your outer mind's ability to guide your life, you give your effort, belief, and energy to the building of your physical resources alone. These come and go as quickly as the currents of the ocean re-arrange the sandy shores of the beach. You may go through many experiences over and over, with the same types of people, with the same attitudes and beliefs, unaware that to break the cycle is to put attention on your spiritual resources. The full measure of your effectiveness, love, and endurance through challenge and struggle is found through awakening your spirit. Your spirit is manifested love. It holds your intention for meaningful service, your capacity to overcome adversity, and your ability to see beauty, compassion, and joy where there may seem to be none. You become a creator, a divine initiator, when you know your own awakened spirit.

SPIRITUAL OPPORTUNITY

The guidance coming to you through this intense and powerful image is to show you that specific obstacles may be in your life in order to clear the way for greater spiritual wisdom, physical success, and prosperity. Something that you care passionately about may seem to be in jeopardy: a relationship may seem to be breaking up, or an opportunity for abundance may seem to be evaporating. The red/orange colors of this flower's pistil and stamen show you that you are dealing with an issue that is core to your life. Orange is the color of the balance you seek and red the passion of your emotions that have been aroused. You may, for example, be ready to talk things over with parents, children, or those who you've felt have stood in your way or hurt you in the past. You may be ready to accept responsibility for a past transgression so you can release guilt and advance into a more accepting outlook.

The aspects of this flower are meant to help you appreciate the significant nature of the issues you are addressing in order to have the courage to persevere. You are moving long-standing blocks out of your path so that you may move dramatically onward into success and abundance.

APPLICATION

When you feel yourself on a threshold of change or choice and are unsure what to do, try praying, "Dear guardian angel, please allow me to benefit from this change and to know the course of action I should take. Allow my guidance to be shown to me in such direct and obvious ways that I can be at peace, knowing I won't overlook or fail to see the guideposts. Let my intention for service and right choices be heard clearly, and let me trust that what comes to me will benefit my life appropriately."

Introspection

29

Introspection

PRESENT CHALLENGE
**Appreciating that Nature is teaching you to value
life as a spiritual process.**

You have drawn this card because you have entered a period
of rapid internal spiritual change. These changes may be
manifesting in your life as an insatiable desire to read and
learn from books, a longing to travel, or perhaps a desire to
move or vacation in places offering a very different landscape.

Your shifting internal landscape may also be recognizable
through sudden mood shifts or the abrupt emergence of ideas,
compulsions, feelings, or desires that are entirely new to you.
Energy is on the move in your being, and Nature is the cata-
lyst to help you learn. This card comes to tell you that Nature
has an important gift for you that will encourage your spiritual
awakening.

ANGELIC MESSAGE
Introspection

*The Planet Earth is specifically a reality of choice. Each day, each
moment, you are presented with choices. The planet is primarily
water, and water is symbolic of transforming the spirit, searching
for God within. Your body is also largely water, and so without*

any effort on your part, your life is destined for spiritual awakening because all your choices lead inevitably toward the spiritual realm.

Humanity's process of spiritual awakening is coming to a head as Nature seeks to touch those compassionate humans who understand their relationship to all living things. Humanity needs to regulate its activities and, in so doing, to be able to re-establish meaningful and lasting relationships with the natural orders of life. You are part of this process, being further awakened yourself and also seeking to awaken others to function in desirable stewardship roles.

You are aware that you have choices in your life even if you are unaware of the spiritual basis of these choices. When you look deeply into any aspect of Nature—any animal, plant, or tree, for instance—you may wonder what choices these living things have. Nature's choices involve either growing toward or away from close ties with humankind. But these choices may take many years to manifest. Human choices, by contrast, can change the planet in a matter of moments or a few years. Nature has little control in the short term over the choices that humanity makes even when these choices portend disaster. Nature is vulnerable to external predators—namely, humanity. Humanity is vulnerable to internal predators: its own fear and lack of spiritual presence.

We, your angelic teachers, are suggesting that you and all of humanity are vulnerable to both positive and negative change. When you recognize feelings of love for Nature waking up inside you, you have heard Nature's urgent pleas to help create a mutually supportive, lasting physical and spiritual environment. You are being asked to accept Nature's gift of a shared future, and you are being urged to awaken to the needs of the life around you.

SPIRITUAL OPPORTUNITY

The guidance coming to you through this flower image is to open to the full presence and power of your life and to accept your role as a steward of the Earth. You are being encouraged to unfold into the full and glorious nature of your life as this flower is doing symbolically. You are being urged to listen to your heart and to observe life around you in order to sense the true significance of the choices being asked of you.

Nature is seeking to teach you primarily to be observant of the subtle as well as the obvious. As the ant, caterpillar, butterfly, or field mouse must continually sense and observe its environment for predators, you also are required to continually observe your internal environment for predators. Your predators are a lack of attention to the quality of your life, a lack of love in making choices that affect Nature's well-being, a preoccupation with your own needs regardless of the cost to other living things, and/or a lack of compassion and respect for all life. You are being urged to truly observe your own inner nature as part of the larger natural world you are being called upon to protect.

APPLICATION

Train yourself to look closely at life, absorbing both the positive and the negative, the life-enhancing and the life-diminishing. Choose a plant or an animal and watch it for fifteen minutes. If you are observing a plant, become that plant in your imagination. Imagine you have petals, buds, and roots. Close your eyes and feel your roots reaching out into the soil and your leaves opening to the fresh air and sunshine. Imagine you have bloomed and that now your life force is being withdrawn back into your essence. Notice the changes you feel through this introspective process.

If you choose to watch an animal, try to imagine what it would feel like to be that animal. Try holding your attention in the same way as the animal does. Relish the food you eat. Try walking with stealth and caution. Wait, watch, and listen with all your senses focused on a subtle movement. As you open your imagination to these other life forms, you become more observant of the subtle shifts in your own life.

Desire

30

30

Desire

PRESENT CHALLENGE
Healing yourself by healing your relationship with the spirit of Nature.

You have drawn this card to help you prioritize time for your own healing and for relaxation away from the commitments and responsibilities of your life.

This card of Rejuvenation offers you permission to allow your own inner child to come forth, bringing with him or her your spontaneity, inquisitiveness, and enjoyment in rediscovering your appreciation for yourself and the world around you. You may have become so preoccupied with trying to make your business successful, or meeting the needs of your family, friends or spouse, or trying to change and heal your life, that you're forgetting the importance of laughter, joy, and temporary freedom from responsibility. This card is offering that you may need to take time for yourself to relax and re-balance your life.

ANGELIC MESSAGE
Desire

Each human being has a natural passion and desire for living. This desire is often smothered through the struggles and traumas of daily life and the apparent lack of time to accomplish and enjoy life fully.

Desire is a part of human nature, and it is often a good thing to turn the energy of desire away from mere sexual fulfillment or task-oriented accomplishment toward accepting the energy of desire as the urge to return and reconnect with nature. You and Nature will both benefit from time together, and healing will be facilitated in both of you.

We, your angelic teachers, refer to healing as more than healing the body or the mind, although these are both important. The larger level of healing we speak of involves healing the relationship between your spirit and the spirit of the Earth. As you come to the Earth with your desire to appreciate her presence, you sustain her in her own changing patterns. As you seek to honor Nature and value her creatures, you give her permission to live her own life purpose fully. Planet Earth has a life purpose, as you do, and that purpose involves bringing all levels of life together into a harmonious and self-appreciating balance. When humankind is unable to honor and acknowledge Earth, she experiences the pain of imbalance, and her own spiritual desire is thwarted.

When you take time to relax in Nature, find a place that is peaceful and fills you with love for yourself and for life. When you are quiet you are able to feel more readily the Earth's own spirit, and through this subtle attention you encourage her to care for the creatures living on the Earth. When you show compassion to the spirit of Earth, you not only enhance your own ability to relate to Nature, you also increase her ability to relate to you and all of humanity. Your desire to seek a deeper exchange with Nature encourages her spirit and further balances all levels of life, continuing the viability of your Earth-School environment.

SPIRITUAL OPPORTUNITY

The guidance coming to you through this flower image is that in order for you to truly appreciate your own desires you need to understand your life against the larger picture of the Natural World. The extraordinary diversity represented in this flower shows you symbolically both the complexities of all living things and the smooth and consistent energy of Nature at large.

The white color of perfection and the red and pink colors of passion and love are all woven together in this image to guide you into a greater appreciation of your own inner nature and the Natural World of which you are an important part. This card is suggesting that in order to stay balanced and healthy you need to participate in Nature with your own basic nature fully alert and ready to participate.

APPLICATION

A few moments focused on a natural element or devoted to time in Nature can offer you refreshment. Look out the window at the blowing leaves. Walk outside and find a flower to talk to. Let there be quiet times within each hour when you pull your energy back inside and let it refresh your body. Your spirit learns from Nature, so when you seek refreshment and rejuvenation, seek out the flowers, plants, trees, and animals who can take your mind off your daily activities and give your spirit a deeper appreciation for its own daily tasks.

Reconnect with Nature a few moments every waking hour for one week, and notice the new levels of energy you have for all aspects of your living.

Relaxation

31

Relaxation

PRESENT CHALLENGE
Rediscovering your inner nature through observation of physical nature.

You have drawn this card to give yourself permission to take time for yourself in a natural environment in order to refill your inner reservoirs and to reacquaint yourself with your inner nature.

You are being guided to build confidence in your ability to make the right choices for yourself, your family and friends, and your life work. This is a Rejuvenation card and seeks to encourage you to look at the bigger picture of life through relationship with Nature. Even though you may feel over-burdened by the demands of your life, you can still take time for yourself because it is essential to your ability ultimately to meet your life goals.

ANGELIC MESSAGE
Relaxation

Relaxation is half the equation for a meaningful life and is the complement to focused attention and constriction. When either half of the relaxation/constriction life-supportive equation is eroded, the human body and psyche suffers. In order to remain spiritually alert, you are required to do more than to meditate in a vacuum. You have incarnated into an exquisitely beautiful natural environment. Your spiritual identity is tied to the other living things that support your daily life. Just as the animals, plants, trees, and minerals each seek to complete their own meaningful life cycles that are based in spiritual evolution, so do you.

Observing the beauty of Nature with more than a vacant stare gives you further practice in the spiritual skill of discovery through paying attention. Consider the flower petals that without fear of death, without strain of being other than they are, without tension and with joy, relax into their fullest expression of beauty. Going into Nature with awareness is different from going blankly and unthinkingly or unfeelingly into Nature. Nature is as alive as you are and benefits from your insightful interactions just as humans benefit from Nature's wisdom.

You might ask, "In what ways can I learn from Nature?" Consider the skill of observation. When you observe the most intricate and minute processes of life, you value and appreciate your own unseen processes that keep you alive. When you revel in the giant and inexplicable majesty of a vast natural landscape that may include mountains or an ocean, you elevate your understanding of yourself as equally complex and inexplicable and also created through divine intention.

Nature is your shadow and your teacher, reflecting back to you the opposite sides of your own personality and spirit. Seeking nature's truths for your life through quiet appreciation offers you an important view of your own life as tied to Nature's support systems and in turn to the spiritual support system of the Universe.

SPIRITUAL OPPORTUNITY

The guidance coming to you through this flower is to recognize that all activity is essentially spiritual at its center. When you seek to have fun and find refreshment, take a few moments to recognize and honor your own spirit and the spirit within every other living thing. Notice that the white center of this lovely purple flower is also tinged with purple, asking you to consider that all the activities that you pursue in your life are tied together, meshed into one interrelated spiritual fabric that supports all life.

When you go into the yard, the park, or the woods; or when you plant a bulb, a flower, or a tree; or when you rescue an animal, free an insect, rebuild or honor nature in any way, you are responding to the Earth's spirit in all life. Through time spent in Nature you find images to draw from, images that inspire you in any daily journal writing you do, in painting, pottery, sculpture, jewelry-making, or any creative endeavor. The eternal shapes, colors, and juxtapositions of objects will offer you a continuing source of enjoyment. You'll be able to bask in the beauty of these remembered images and scenes from Nature, and these experiences will help you keep your own creative impulses alive in your life when you return home to normal routines.

APPLICATION

Select one specific aspect of Nature to teach you something important today. Follow this aspect throughout the day, paying attention to the difference stages of contraction or relaxation it experiences. Because the elements of Nature are alive and you are alive, you share a common bond and can come to "hear" each other through your heart and your perception. Do you understand what the trees are saying as the forest whispers through the wind blowing in its branches? Do you know what all the excitement is about when the squawking birds swoop down from a nearby tree? Could you know, if you took the time to learn, the art of "non-thinking" and "staying present" through simple observation? In order to benefit from relaxation you are being encouraged to experience your life as bonded to all other living things and, through this realization of connectedness, to absorb the active living energy Nature puts forth to refocus and heal your life.

Freedom

32

32

Freedom

PRESENT CHALLENGE
Turning your impatience into spiritual energy for self-discovery through Nature.

You have drawn this card as a means of finding a more satisfying inner freedom from anxiety and feelings of being pushed by life, with never enough time, energy, money, or experience to find or create what you feel you need or are ready for.

You may feel impatient with other people or with your own spiritual progress. You may feel impatient with your work, lack of work, or inability to find or create meaningful work. You may feel impatient to heal. This card has the energy of investigation and urges you to discover the freedom exhibited by Nature as each living thing goes about its own activities.

ANGELIC MESSAGE
Freedom

One of the greatest delusions of Earth School is that there is only limited time in which to accomplish your goals and meet your essential needs. You may have limited ordinary mental time, but you have unlimited spiritual time, and this is an essential difference to become aware of when seeking freedom from struggle and stress.

Your ordinary mind has you rushing headlong toward death, with hardly an opportunity to breathe in the goodness of life and to benefit from your life before it is over. You can learn freedom from impatience, which means experiencing and expressing the joy and peace of your existence when you break through impatience. When you are impatient you are expressing the ordinary mind's desire to override and shortcut the essential spiritual change and growth process underway within your spirit. Your normal mind tells you not to bother waiting, that you are ready for whatever it is you want right now. If this were so, then you would have done that very thing already, or be doing it this moment. If the goal you want is still outside your reach, then consider that it is also outside your realization. To reach a goal means first to fully realize the nature of what you want and the ways in which it is tied to the very important spiritual process of transformation underway in your life right now.

What is the relationship between impatience and realization? Impatience blocks realization by preventing you from perceiving the natural confluence of experience and spiritual understanding merging inside your life. All lasting and meaningful change is arrived at slowly, as you discover that all meaningful opportunities come to you in creating the spiritual realization of these opportunities. Impatience is misleading, because you hear your mind telling you that you are ready for something when you may not be. Nature is never hurried; it responds to the cycles that build, one from the next, as each has fulfilled its opportunity for growth. You are no less guided by the Divine. You too are opening to your opportunities as you observe and work with awareness of your developing spirit.

SPIRITUAL OPPORTUNITY

The guidance coming to you through this flower image is that self-realization lies in experiencing fully each singular aspect of your living. The creamy stamen of this flower lies in the foreground, asking you symbolically to hold your attention on the experiences of the moment. This guidance suggests you need to experience the freedom of this moment. In order to discover joy in the moment and to experience the freedom to take the time you need for the people and individual experiences in your life, pay attention to occasions when the opposite is true and you feel impatient.

Why do you feel impatient with another person when that person repeats himself or herself or fails to make the point that you think is important? Where is your awareness and your tension level when you look at your watch and realize you have five minutes to get to the store before it closes? How do you feel when it rains or snows and you have to shovel or put on extra warm or protective clothing? Impatience becomes a way of life that you may hardly recognize as your motivation for gulping down life without savoring any of it. This is the feeling of always being pushed, out of breath, and reaching for what comes next.

How do you relinquish impatience? By keeping your focus on your inner mind, which tells you all life is moving at its most perfect pace and that you are required to sense this pace and move in harmony with it. When you seek this pace, you relax into freedom, and you find you can enjoy each experience of your life and savor its gift fully.

APPLICATION

Take a deep breath, smile at your compulsiveness and anxiety, and love the fact that you can see these in yourself and not judge that they are bad. They are only the product of your normal mind. Try moving through anxiety the next time you are aware of feeling pushed. Stop what you are doing and say to yourself, "There are no time limitations to my spirit's work, and therefore all that I do will come to fruition at exactly the right moment."

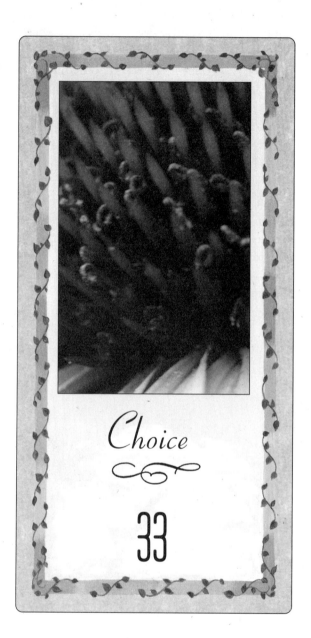

Choice

33

Choice

PRESENT CHALLENGE
Making decisions that reflect reverence for yourself and all other life.

You have drawn this card to help you appreciate the difference between making choices from the perspective of your spirit, your inner mind and being, and making them according to the needs posed by your analytical or outer mind. The calmness and serenity of your life may be obscured by the continual demands made by your outer mind as it seeks to have its needs and desires filled.

You've drawn this important card of Rejuvenation to alert you to the need for greater calmness and inner peace. Although you may work hard at accomplishing the goals you have chosen, in order to find lasting satisfaction you are being called upon to consider the intentions with which you make decisions. You are being guided to consider yourself as part of a vast network of life and responsible for its well-being as well as your own.

ANGELIC MESSAGE
Choice

Making a choice would seem to be a simple matter. And so it is when a life-supportive balance is struck between spiritual freedom and Earth-School responsibility. *Spiritual freedom is the inner aspect of choice that urges you to live as part of an all-encompassing and whole planetary system.* Your spirit understands that all choices must replenish your physical system and the entire ecosystem. You are learning to consider your spirit's perspective so that you can accept greater responsibility for encouraging the restoration of your physical environment.

Nature has no favorites; it loves the frog and the fish equally; it supports the bird and dog in the same ways. And so Nature cares no more for you than for the butterfly or the mountain lion or for the person far away on the other side of your planet. Just as the Creator seeks to perpetuate the physical and nonphysical systems of life, so too is Nature concerned with the whole system of life on Earth.

You and we, your angelic teachers, are each essential parts of the system, neither more nor less. And so each living thing must learn to responsibly exercise its right to draw from the resources of the largest systems of life, accepting that it will need to give back to the Earth and to the Creator. Every living thing ultimately relinquishes its form in order to nourish a larger, everlasting system.

SPIRITUAL OPPORTUNITY

The guidance coming to you through this flower is to fully appreciate your choices as extensions of your spirituality. Symbolically, you can see that you can make choices from either a spiritual perspective or a rational and perhaps self-centered perspective. Notice that in this flower image there is a sharp contrast between the prickly center and the smooth, pink petals. You are guided to realize that each choice you make can help you live in balance with Nature by accepting responsibility for your choices.

When making a choice, it isn't just which option you choose, it is the quality, intention, and commitment from which you choose that course of action that tells you whether or not your spirit is engaged in the decision. As human beings you are not asked, for example, to choose between wealth and poverty but to choose fair exchange from the system for providing necessary and meaningful service. You are not asked to choose between celibacy and sexuality but to create relationships that support mutual giving and receiving of love. You are not asked to choose between eco-spirituality and eco-destruction but rather to establish an honorable means of balancing all needs for life.

This important card has been drawn because you are in need of making choices that more consistently reflect a reverence for yourself and all other life.

APPLICATION

Watch the criteria you tell yourself are important in making choices. When facing a choice, even a small one, first take a deep breath. When you make choices while breathing shallowly, you are using only your outer mind, or "functioning self," not your spirit or inner mind, which allows for full participation.

Ask yourself, "Whom will this choice benefit?" Each choice that has your spirit behind it will benefit you and others equally. Ask yourself, "How easy is it for me to make this choice?" If it is very easy, then consider that perhaps you have only sought to reaffirm those attitudes and beliefs that you already hold. Imagine having to stretch to find a comfort level with a choice that suggests your needs and wants may need to be suspended or altered in order to give or share with others.

Merger

34

34

Merger

PRESENT CHALLENGE
Accepting support from all life to help you bring about the current spiritual evolutionary shift under way.

You have drawn this card of Merger because you may be needing encouragement that your efforts in bringing spiritual awareness into your paid and/or volunteer work is making a difference. You may feel lonely in your work because you seem to be the one always pushing for positive change against the established status quo. You may wonder if you are capable of staying on purpose and empowered in your mission because there seems to be so much resistance to your efforts. You may also be feeling defeated, tired, and/or burned out.

You have drawn this card because you are a light-worker of the twenty-first century. You are being guided to listen to the angels and continue your work because you are hearing guidance that others may not yet appreciate.

ANGELIC MESSAGE
Merger

You have accepted this journey through Earth School in this lifetime because you wanted the challenge of participating in the current evolutionary shift on your planet. You and all of humanity will cause this shift as the individual points of light, those people and groups living in the spiritual energy of love, merge into a powerful healing network. You are part of building and empowering this network of light, and sometimes this is lonely work.

We, your angelic teachers, understand your struggle and also your fears and frustrations. But we also see an expansive future that you may not always believe is possible. Your daily life seems normal enough in its requirements, but you are also being asked to do the extraordinary, to merge with our vision, to live in the guidance of the Creator that speaks to a different, more humane and enlightened planetary home. You are being asked to believe what you are unable to see and what many people may tell you is foolish. You are merging with those on and off the Earth who are guiding your energy because you accept a different future for humanity.

Holding a vision takes energy and effort. So when you feel let down, depressed, or afraid that your abilities and insights are insufficient to the task at hand, talk to Nature. Nature is all around you no matter where on the Earth you live. Nature is all about merger, because it functions as one entirely interwoven system. You, like Nature, are becoming more and more connected with other light-workers in physical and nonphysical reality. Through merger you gain strength and the ability to endure. After all, you know what others may not: that you draw love and comfort from experiencing these bonds. Let us comfort you when you feel unworthy or lacking in any way. Hold out your arms and let us send love into your body and mind so that you may endure, for you are the carriers of the light, the hope of the future.

SPIRITUAL OPPORTUNITY

The guidance coming to you through this flower image is to accept that you and all living things come from a common Source even though you may sometimes question your understanding of this Source. The red petals in this image are curved and in varying states of blooming, symbolic of the state of your various projects. The green stems support the flowers, and for you this translates into accepting and seeking the healing energy flowing from the Creator through Nature and into your life.

You are being guided to believe in the process of change rather than only in goals that are attained. You are being asked to accept that you are already merged with the forces of Creation that are at work in your life and on the planet. Your guidance is to continue to put forth your best efforts and to draw more extensively from the subtle beauty and force of the natural world.

APPLICATION

Nature is persistent. A sidewalk is often cracked by the green grass. Water wears away stone to create a deep gorge. The force of Nature emerges ultimately successful because of its persistence and the energy it draws from others of its kind. One blade of grass or one drop of water has no power, but many blades of grass or many droplets of water together continually change the face of the planet.

To help you draw energy from your entire support system, identify those living things that you feel aligned with and that you know support your efforts and your life. These things can be people, animals, trees, or any other individual or collective aspects of Nature or humanity. Also write out the names of your angelic teachers and guides whom you feel or know are with you, or the names of friends, relatives, or teachers who have passed into spirit. Now place each of these small slips of paper in a basket, and each morning choose one name to accept love from and to send your love to.

Change

35

35

Change

PRESENT CHALLENGE
Accepting that your larger life goal is to grow in grace and find union with all living things.

You have drawn this Rejuvenation card because you may be weary of challenging life and long to have things in your life flow more easily toward love and success.

You may have spent years learning a spiritual discipline, or you may be new to spirituality. In either case you are facing a subtle but powerful spiritual challenge, one requiring you to trust your belief in the God within and to allow the beauty and intensity of this connection to smooth your path in the physical world.

ANGELIC MESSAGE
Change

Change, when it is lived as a sacred process, portends spiritual transformation. All levels of change, no matter how slight or how deeply penetrating or disruptive, have something to show you about your belief in the wisdom of your teachers, masters, and the angelic messengers who sweep through your daily lives. Change wakes you up to life as the spiritual process that it is. Change is different from chance, because change is intended to bring you continually closer to God, while chance is purely the random movement of physical energy. Through change you, like an abundance of flowering blossoms, merge with the wisdom mind of God. You are continually offered the insight and ability to accept the angels drawn to you to heal the fear, pain, and anxiety that separate you from loving yourself as a divine aspect of the God-force.

Change is upsetting because the unknown has no discernible texture, no familiar faces, no assurances of success. When you are unable to ascertain what is coming into your life through the mist of change, it is easy and natural to be afraid. This fear, however, can create an impenetrable barrier to the divine love surging toward convergence into your life. Through change you can come to accept that life on physical Earth is brief and that your journey is always to gaze toward the Divine and to learn of your true divinity. When you feel frightened by life, it helps to understand that you are choosing between a belief in a loving, divine Providence and the randomness of chance happening. Whatever comes to you can be a significant opportunity for spiritual growth, whether it was intended as that or not. Your larger life goal is to grow in grace and to find union with the divine Presence through love.

SPIRITUAL OPPORTUNITY

The guidance coming to you through this image of flowers is to take heart and believe in the significance of the changes taking place in your life. The blossoms, some open and some still closed, speak to the ongoing texture of your life in which some aspects will be known and others will remain elusive. You can also accept that even though not all your life experiences are positive, they all ultimately have a positive resolution. The brilliant white blossoms tell you that all life is created in God's image and that a spiritual value rests in all of your experiences, even those that are painful.

Your spirit is tireless in its loving support and prodding of your life in order to help you move out of your own way so you can find the love you seek. You incarnated into this life to learn and accept the continually changing nature of your life as preparation for the continually changing nature of your eternal reality: life, to death, to merger with the Divine, to life, to death, and again to merger with the Divine.

Your heart or inner mind urges you to give, share, cooperate, love, value, and honor other living things because these are the qualities offered by a loving heart and an awakened spirit. When you are afraid that accepting the present changes in your life will bring you greater pain, fear, loss, or poverty, consider that the opposite is more likely true. Consider that to avoid accepting change and learning from it will produce these undesirable outcomes.

APPLICATION

Think about the changes that you feel are taking shape in the spiritual currents of your life. Are you coming to the realization that, on a deep level, an important relationship is over or shifting in some way, or that you must release your children to their own learning and get on with your life, or that you need to change jobs or life work or to give up some self-defining way of life?

Make a list of these impending changes, and quietly, in each morning's meditation, place your hand over this list and imagine that a brilliant, divine light allows God's loving current to flow through you and out of your hand to bring positive and life-enhancing resolutions to these changes.

Fulfillment

36

36

Fulfillment

PRESENT CHALLENGE
Finding lasting nourishment from your involvement with others and your living environment.

You have drawn this card of Fulfillment to help you find renewed enjoyment and support for your life. In trying to keep pace with your busy lifestyle, you may be eating, drinking, and/or working in ways that fail to nourish you. You may be obsessing about your relationships, your future, or your self-worth to the extent that you have ceased to draw love and fulfillment from your environment.

To keep from burning out and to find renewed support for your life, you are being requested to stop and really look, smell, listen, touch, and hear the people in your life and the beauty and spontaneity of the living things in your environment.

ANGELIC MESSAGE
Fulfillment

When you enjoy being with other people and find pleasure in the beauty of Earth around you, then you are more able to balance your tendency toward addictions because you are living at a deeper feeling level—a spiritual level. At the level of your spirit you accept that you are only one part of the entire physical and nonphysical system. Addictions are mental, not spiritual. And when you have walled yourself off from feelings or have so focused your attention on personal needs and personal achievements that you fail to receive the gifts of life, then it is easy to find the substances that replace the natural spiritual fulfillment.

When the rational parts of your mind become too dominant, your entire focus stays trained on your own needs and accomplishments. You find every activity in your life becoming stressful, competitive, and unfulfilling. This is because you believe that you are responsible for, or being required to change, everything that you come in contact with to fit your own needs and requirements. Try engaging in a conversation without judging what is said, only enjoying what takes place. See how long you can keep your attention on anything other than your own reaction and responses. Lasting fulfillment comes from accepting other living things and enjoying their offerings without the need to change or alter them.

Addictions are unnecessary when you allow the feelings, sensations, and enjoyment of your living to nourish and fulfill you. Imagine that you are living on the moon and that the landscape includes nothing green or living. You are all alone. When you are caught in an addictive pattern, this is symbolically the way in which you feel. You feel walled off from life, from love, from understanding, and from nourishment.

The opposite of addiction is involvement in life and the ability to see and accept beauty in its natural state. To overcome addiction, help yourself appreciate that you are with other people to enjoy them and with the natural world to accept its grace without needing to change it. When you take time to engage life, ready to absorb, participate, and experience rather than change, adjust, or alter it, then you are able to accept the genuine nourishment that life offers you.

SPIRITUAL OPPORTUNITY

The guidance to you from this card is that you will benefit from accepting the authentic aspects of yourself and others and from doing the things that bring you into contact with beauty. The many shades of pink and purple in this flower show you the unlimited variations of love and beauty that are available to you to support your spirit and thus your life. You are being guided to seek the natural complexities and inter-connections of life that cause you to accept your life as only one part of a larger whole.

You are asked to consider your addictions as a call for your spirit to take charge and allow you to participate in life rather than needing always to change it. Accept, believe in yourself, find love, and breathe in the goodness around you that nour-ishes your soul. You need to find fulfillment so that you do not burn out or continue to feel that you must accomplish everything all by yourself.

APPLICATION

Fulfillment comes from the ease of making choices that have become a way of life. For one day, pay particular attention to the things you do that bring you a variety of satisfactions. Ask yourself what part of you feels fulfilled when your spouse, friend, or colleague at work appreciates you and/or your work. In what way do you feel fulfilled when you wash the car, vacu-um the house, or wash the dishes? While these levels of ful-fillment are important, they fail to fill the empty place in your life that needs to wonder at the unknown or accept commu-nity with other life, including God.

Put yourself in an environment that you find beautiful and that fills you on inner levels—an art museum, a botanical gar-den, a library, an aquarium. Each of these allows you to experi-ence a sense of wonder at the nature of life. These experiences of beauty ultimately nourish your spirit and your life.

Attention

37

37

Attention

PRESENT CHALLENGE
Using divine love to transform the worry, fear, or guilt from your shadow side.

You've drawn this card to encourage you to accept without judgment your life, your abilities, and your vulnerabilities. You are being guided to seek to know yourself without fear or resistance to your shadow side, the energy of the night, because it is only the complement to the day and the light awakening within you.

This is a card of release, freedom, and redirected inner energy meant to help you heal emotionally and grow spiritually by encouraging you to value the meaningful experiences in your life while being mindful that each physical lifetime is over all too quickly. This is a powerful card of change and transformation, and you are being shown the means to absorb old emotional energy and convert it into spiritual energy.

ANGELIC MESSAGE
Attention

While you remain in physical life, your shadow side is only half your total being. You are well aware that you have an enlightened

189

side that you seek to expand and share with the world. But aspects of your personality that emerge from fear, greed, jealousy, anger, or resistance are often pushed aside in the hope that they will disappear on their own or will be healed through emotional and/or intellectual practices. You may spend a great deal of energy avoiding and periodically confronting these undesirable personality traits before discovering that you can release them only when you love them.

In accepting that you have tried to live according to your beliefs to the best of your ability and in partnership with the Universe, you can let go of feeling responsible for past actions or inactions. You can accept the opportunity of this moment by placing your attention on the power of divine love to transform all unrealized or negative energy into positive energy of purpose.

One of the most difficult fears for humanity to overcome is the fear of physical death. Today, at this moment, your life is in your hands, and by placing your attention on divine love you are able to overcome even the fear of death. No fear is too large and no personality too unenlightened to be transformed by divine love. Keep your attention this day on your shadow self and/or the shadow qualities of those you love. In your prayers and meditations, bring these into the light; through love, they can be released and transformed into the power of meaningful living.

SPIRITUAL OPPORTUNITY

The guidance to you through this flower image is to seek the healing love of your center—your spirit—and merge it with the universal center—God. The translucent green center of this flower image helps you visualize the power of divine love to heal. Notice that the petals of the flower are purple, the color of spiritual transformation, and they are tipped with the same shade of green as the center. This means that your life is always capable of being transformed through love.

You are being guided to believe in yourself and know that all aspects of your life that you need to change can be changed through love. Because this is a card of Nourishment, you are being asked to release troublesome habits that deal with such physical addictions as addiction to food. Try, for instance, bringing your chewing and swallowing into the focus of divine love as a means of truly nourishing your body and life. If each time you swallow you do so with care and love for yourself and the nutrients you send into your system, then food obsessions as well as all others stand a chance of being transformed.

APPLICATION

Breathing is used in many spiritual practices as a means of focusing attention on a process that brings your life energy into balance and also cleanses your system by eliminating unwanted and negative or unproductive thoughts and feelings. Paying attention to your breathing encourages you to find and renew your intimate relationship with your body and spirit each second of each day. Practice accepting divine love with each breath and releasing and transforming through love every unwanted feeling or pain that you or those you love are burdened with. Some day, when you no longer need to breathe physically, you will leave your physical body supported by the spiritual energy of divine love. But for the moment, keep your attention on the beauty and opportunity available to you through this magical and tenuous process of living.

Encouragement

38

38

Encouragement

PRESENT CHALLENGE
Believing in your healing even when it seems as if you are falling back into old obsessions.

You have drawn this card to reinforce your belief in yourself and your ability to change and heal your life. You may feel as if the old fears and obsessions are gaining strength again because your inner assurance and self-confidence may be slightly shaken by some recent event.

This is a time when you may need to face the transforming of your old patterns by yourself, since friends may be withdrawn into their own concerns. You are being guided to understand that you can do whatever is required to heal because you have invoked divine love to help you begin a new life. You are ready for improved physical health, for relationships with people who are themselves healthier and more capable of sustaining a relationship with you, and for the means to be of service and to value yourself.

ANGELIC MESSAGE
Encouragement

Transformation is the process of healing your separation from God. And although you think your problems stem from rejection, aban-

donment, or trauma at the hands of other people, you are actually facing your desire to release fear and accept love from yourself and from God. Encourage yourself in your efforts to persevere with these positive changes. Continue your meditations and empowering inner work, and you will come into the safe and peaceful waters of divine love.

You might wonder why you are experiencing resistance to the positive changes and repatternings that you are trying to affect in your efforts to heal. The resistance comes from working to abandon your fears rather than continuing to fear being abandoned. Your outer mind, your rational self, has served you well in the past by helping you put aside the memory of painful experiences so that you could meet new people and try again to find love. But this mental programming is presently sabotaging your efforts to re-awaken these old feelings in order to heal rather than erase them.

You may have decided to love yourself, all of you this time, even including the parts that lay deeply hidden. You may be deciding that even the fearful obsessions and inner anger is only your small child inside crying out to be loved and held. So place your arms around your body and feel the love from us, your angelic teachers. We understand your pain and also seek your healing. You are needed on the Earth, and you have the ability to heal through love.

SPIRITUAL OPPORTUNITY

The guidance coming to you through this image is for you to persevere in your efforts to grow spiritually and to transform fear into love. The white perfection of this flower image tells you that all change is possible when seen in the light of divine perfection. The center path of gold leading into the depths of the flower is symbolic of your life path of awakening and taking you into the heart of the Universe.

This guidance is suggesting that every healing path leads ultimately toward God but that you are requested to choose a single path of spiritual study and to stay for the time being with this focus. You are being encouraged to resist the temptation to stop and start your spiritual study, or to switch spiritual teachers, or to alter your present regimen. You have entered a time of perseverence and self-encouragement in order to nourish your life and yourself.

APPLICATION

Your mind and your spirit both vie for your attention during the day. In order to practice giving your spirit and its loving attitude priority, try this exercise. Choose a specific day and begin with a short centering meditation, with your eyes either open or closed. Merely accept that you are loved and are capable of generating love in every corner of your life and with every person. Keep this "I-am-growing-in-love" attitude in your day; try to keep it in your heart as you interact with friends and family and with colleagues at work. To remind yourself that you are seeking to maintain this loving attitude, place an object on the counter or on your desk, and every time you look at it, remind yourself that you are loved. Reaffirm this love for yourself all the way through the day at least once every hour.

How do you feel by nightfall? How difficult has it been to take your attention from what you were doing or thinking and to place it on love? Each time you feel unloving toward yourself or others, place your hand over your heart and reawaken your divine connection.

Cooperation

39

Cooperation

PRESENT CHALLENGE
Seeking love as the means of balancing your life.

You have drawn this card to alert you that the relationship among your body, mind, and spirit is ready to reach a more refined level of inner cooperation.

You may have worked extensively to overcome old feelings of abuse, neglect, abandonment, loss, or low self-worth. You may be finding that even with all the inner-child work, the spiritual alignment work, body work, or other spiritual approaches to healing you've tried, you still feel blocked in some significant way from your desired state of inner well-being. This blockage is giving way to a subtle level of cooperation of body, mind, and spirit that is emerging into your life to improve your self-confidence and to awaken your soul-confidence.

ANGELIC MESSAGE
Cooperation

Cooperation is essential for the systems of your body to maintain your life. Life is interesting, stimulating, fun, sensual, and fulfilling on many levels as you interact with those you love, dislike, fear, or feel competitive with. Even the chemical responses of your body are linked directly to specific emotions. Clearly, the body, mind, and emotions have a close alignment.

Your spirit's purpose is to facilitate cooperation between you and Gaia, the Earth, and between you and God. Through these avenues of receiving and experiencing the profound feelings of love, your body and emotions are able to respond to love as a transcendent quality. When you accept your relationship with God and thus with divine love, you become a channel for profound compassion, kindness, goodness, and nonjudgement, just as every spiritual seeker does. When you seek the energy of love you rise above the lesser emotional responses and are supported in your ability to act and think nobly.

Cooperation between your feelings and your body create physical health and feelings of happiness and fulfillment. Cooperation among your feelings, your body, and your spirit gives you the ability to experience the grace of God as love and to interpret the energy of love as the guidance you seek. The spiritual energy of love is arising from the divine Presence and raises you to the status of inspired mortal and wise healer of other living things.

Experiencing cooperation at the subtle levels of love puts you in touch with the place of true nourishment; for no matter how many people you have in your life, if you are missing a connection to God, the immortal energy of love, you will feel empty, alone, and finite. You are growing in wisdom to accept the urge to seek cooperation externally with other people and internally among your own body, mind, and spirit. Cooperation is essential to balancing your life with the Sacred in all things.

SPIRITUAL OPPORTUNITY

The guidance to you through this flower image is to search within yourself to discover those ways in which you are testing yourself and God. The brilliant gold and orange in this image offers the potential for splendid change, healing, and renewed balance. The dark anthers that hold the pollen at the end of the brilliant waving stamens in this flower image suggest that you are holding within you a disclarity, ambivalence, or nonessential belief about the way in which God is present in your life.

You are learning to listen to the Universe and to interpret these impressions to guide your life. Are you still tossing down the gauntlet to God, asking why things aren't better in your life right now? Are you playing a wait-and-see game with God before committing completely to a spiritual path? This guidance is suggesting that you will benefit from asking yourself what miracle or dramatic event will be necessary for you to believe that you are in close alignment with God. This card is suggesting that such an occurrence may be coming to you to prove to you that you have a genuine relationship with God.

APPLICATION

Consider that, in order to experience the inner cooperation described above, you need to understand and work with the vibrations that are coming into your body and mind with each second of each day. Each of these sensory experiences can be deepened to pick up your spirit's love before returning through the words you speak.

Strike a bell, tuning fork, or single note on a musical instrument, or imagine a clear and profound note reverberating through you. Then say your name to yourself several times, and imagine that each time you say your name and strike a note, the vibrations of the sound carry your name deep into your heart. Finally, during conversations with others, imagine that each thought travels from your brain through your heart before being spoken through your lips. This simple exercise reminds you that you are capable of facilitating a deeply cooperative attitude within your own life and within the lives of others.

Joy

40

40

Joy

PRESENT CHALLENGE
Experiencing inner freedom and the expectation of positive occurrences.

You have drawn this card because you want to feel free and released from burden. You may feel that you always did what others wanted and played by the rules as others set them. But now you realize you've sacrificed a great deal of your own creativity and individuality and have been afraid to tackle some of the things you might have wanted to try. No longer afraid of failure or the judgements of others, you are ready to spread your wings and discover qualities, abilities, and inner strengths that have been trying to emerge.

You have drawn this card because you are being guided to continue to believe in yourself and to seek success as it is emerging in your life, often in unexpected and unforeseen ways and events.

ANGELIC MESSAGE
Joy

Joy is closely aligned with freedom because the joyful human being experiences life's fullness and nurturing even through disappoint-

ment, anger, anxiety, or loss. Joy is an internal state of being, one that emerges from a profound belief in the sacredness of life. If you are moving into joy, it is because you have accepted that you can risk. Whether or not you succeed in the terms you imagine, you have succeeded in the eyes of the Universe. When you risk saying, doing, or expressing your own essence, you become renewed even when you are initially uncomfortable or afraid of being vulnerable or feeling exposed. You are moving into self-love and confidence.

Joy is the natural state of the spiritually-ordered person. Joy is the inner understanding that all things are held in the loving embrace of God and the angels and that a meaningful explanation and/or learning will emerge that will ultimately benefit us all.

Joy comes from all of the company of heaven who sing your praises when you rise to an important occasion and invest in others emotionally because you believe in yourself. You are mortal for only a moment in time, and each of these moments, though brief, has a purpose: to deepen your acceptance of life beyond physical life.

Here is a prayer from a human heart; perhaps you will recognize your own feelings in it: "Dear Heavenly Teachers, allow me to believe in the rightness and goodness of life even when I see too much of the opposite. Permit me to bring love into the world even when my first response is to doubt love. Accept my life as a means of service to the Universe so that joy may abound on Earth and within each living thing."

SPIRITUAL OPPORTUNITY

You have drawn this flower image to encourage the awakening of love and joy in your life. You are being guided to believe in yourself and in your dreams because you are entering a powerful and extremely positive period in your life when you will see some of your deepest desires come to fruition.

The deep pink and rose of this flower image shows you that when you believe in love and accept life's lessons as teachers, you ultimately gain in wisdom and contentment. This card is one of the cards of Nourishment because it comes to reassure you that you are being reborn into a lasting relationship with joy. It is a healing card and can be used to further your own physical healing and to transfer healing energy to others. Breathe in the essence of joy you feel after reading the guidance offered through this card. Then, as you breathe out, repeat the name of the person, yourself or someone else, whom you wish to receive this powerful energy.

APPLICATION

Practice feeling joy. Look in the mirror at your mouth and expression. What do you see? Are the lines in your face set in the patterns of tenderness, good humor, and compassion? Move your mouth and expression into a frown to reflect worry, concern, frustration, and anger. Which expression are you more familiar with?

Life can offer you no inner peace until you determine to accept it for yourself. Tomorrow will be no different from today. In this moment lies the opportunity to peel off the layers that burden you and accept your natural state of joy. Write the word "JOY" on a piece of paper and put it in your pocket or purse. Carry it with you as a reminder of what you are choosing. Rather than remaining hostage to life's changes, expect understanding and continued joy to flow to you—and it will.

Healing

41

41

Healing

PRESENT CHALLENGE
Awakening to the healer within you.

You have drawn this card of Healing because you are being awakened to the healer within you wanting and needing to emerge.

You may be hearing the Earth's spirit calling you or feeling that you hear ringing in your ears humanity's hunger to find peace. Your own spirit's compassion may be calling you to participate in this time of planetary change, and it is essential to your own healing that you heed this call.

Your guidance is to believe in your own emerging feelings and capabilities and to accept that the future you want will emerge only as you see the ways in which you are already doing your healing work. You are asked to take heart and to believe in yourself as a healer with the God-given capacity to engage your eyes, your hands, and your heart to be of service.

ANGELIC MESSAGE
Healing

Healing means more than reaching out and touching someone, although this act does produce physical and emotional healing.

Healing is the process of revitalizing yourself and other living things through divine love. When you seek to heal yourself you are really asking to become aware of the influence you exert on others and they on you and your life.

The path of the spiritual searcher, which is to be a healer in some form, is first to experience personally the mystical opening to God and then to allow this wisdom to flow out into the world as a healing agent. Because you are already experiencing God in some way, you are seeking to allow your healing potential to become known to others in order to use your ability to improve conditions on or within the Earth. We, your angelic teachers, understand this natural spiritual progression and are helping you awaken and enhance your own unconditional love in order to become the planetary citizen you wish to be.

Love is the energy of the Divine. Whenever it is invoked or even allowed to be drawn into your relationships, both people and other living things benefit. Whenever you contribute love to any situation or relationship, you are not only healing yourself and others involved in the immediate conversation, you are contributing to your planet a lasting effect of love and sustained peace.

Love is the common denominator of all living experiences. When you apply love without judgement or expectation, you always produce a healing result. Whenever you place your hands, actually or symbolically, on another living thing, for example, a healing is forthcoming in the most appropriate way. As you awaken your love as a planetary being, you will feel increasing passion to alleviate the plight of other living things. This is good, and it will ultimately be the means of healing Earth.

SPIRITUAL OPPORTUNITY

The guidance available to you through this flower image is to recognize the essential center of your life—your spirit and its ability to offer unconditional love and acceptance to yourself and all other living things. Notice the center of this flower and its brilliance, which represents the universal essence or core of all life. Your life, like this flower, has an essential center. Through awareness of your spiritual core, you are able to draw divine realization into every aspect of your life to benefit all life.

You are being guided to realize that even though you may be experiencing "roadblocks" or "caution signs" in the pursuit of your work as a healing agent, you are being asked only to believe enough in yourself and your connection to the Divine through love to see that you are already doing, in some small way, the important work that you hope to expand. Rather than believing that your opportunities lie in the future, dependent upon other people or circumstances, accept that you are meant to do this work now and are in fact working for planetary well-being at this very moment. Bring the force of your healing capability, your passion, and your skill to bear on those people and circumstances presently in your life. In this way the people, finances, and opportunities you need will find you.

APPLICATION

Close your eyes and imagine that your spirit is a brilliant white star, just like the center of the flower image on this card. Now, in your mind's eye, place this white star on any part of your physical body or any part of the physical Earth that needs healing. Imagine that this perfect reflection of divine love is pulsating with love, pumping it into that organ or into that country or into that hurting place on the Earth.

Imagery is effective in moving the energy of love to various needed locations. You can perform this exercise any time you see something or someone who needs help. Call up this image of divine perfection and unconditional love to support your healing efforts.

Sustenance

42

$\mathcal{S}$ustenance

PRESENT CHALLENGE
*Merging your guidance from your angelic teachers to help
you love yourself.*

You have drawn this card to improve your ability to hear and participate in work with your angelic teachers and, in so doing, to feel more secure in relationships with other people who are less committed to following a spiritual path.

You are needing to sustain your body and maintain your inner balance more completely and thoroughly as you surmount the challenges and accept the changes in your life. You may feel you've been too heavily influenced by the opinions and actions of others and that you are now seeking to stay within your own power and find your love for yourself, so that you can grow spiritually even if others choose not to.

ANGELIC MESSAGE
Sustenance

You may not think of angels as supporting your life as directly as we do, but the angelic realm is committed to helping each human being in many specific ways to transform current personal and planetary difficulties. We seek to enlighten humanity to move more completely into a course of wise action stemming from a creative involvement with us and with all inspired teachers of love and compassion. We are ever-present to you as a source of solace and enduring support. We are in your dreams by night and your meditations by day. We are always with you through pain or loss, through death and transcendence, and through joy, health, recovery, and lasting success.

You speak to us and we speak to you most directly through the beauty of flowers on your Earth. The flowers are our angelic messengers, meant to offer you our love and support. When you look into the face of a flower you see the Universe, the galaxies, the stars, and the planets sprinkled and clustered across the sky. You see life, death, and re-birth. You see human frailty, fear, and loss as well as courage, joy, and ascension.

Working with flower images will help you develop your intuition and your ability to more readily interpret your life symbolically and archetypically. Guidance is everywhere around you. As you accept that you and we are one, then the fact that you are for the moment physical and we are for the time being spiritual will present no barriers to our being together.

We speak to you through flowers so that you can draw essential help and love for your own life. There are lessons to be learned by observing flowers. You can hear us each day, each moment, and benefit from closing the space between your heart and our love, between your point of transformation and our assurance of your eternal life.

SPIRITUAL OPPORTUNITY

The guidance being shared with you through this flower image asks you to focus on the power of challenge and the importance of lessons learned. Notice, in this image, the striking white center representing God and the angels reaching out to you. The dark circle beneath the light center portrays the potentially stressful, fearful, or anxiety-producing nature of daily living. Yet the magnificent color of rose permeating the petals—and, symbolically, your life—suggests that you benefit from listening in love to your spirit and your teachers. As you grow through challenges to your physical health and the continued well-being and growth in your relationships, your spirit is sustaining and strengthening you and encouraging your acceptance of lasting well-being.

You are more effective, productive, and capable of love yourself when you seek and live the guidance that is so continually available to you through flowers. You will be more successful in finding happiness in your own partnership or close relationships as you accept your own spiritual center and seek to know it better. If others talk behind your back or misrepresent your motives, or if people you love seem to wobble and vacillate emotionally and seem unable to offer you what you need, understand that they too are seeking a spiritual center, whether they are able to verbalize that search or not. Unconditional love for self and others, fairness, compassion, understanding, lack of judgement—all are qualities that emerge when individuals are sustained by their spirit and they know it.

APPLICATION

An important part of living and loving purposefully is to be aware of bringing your spiritual insight into the circumstances of everyday living. The next time you have an upsetting or incomplete conversation, one that leaves you feeling unsettled, ask yourself, "What should I take in from this conversation that can help me? What belief about myself is being challenged? What am I willing to admit about myself and the other person without judging the rightness or wrongness of either my response or that of the other person?"

The Angels love you for your potential and your persistence in reaching meaningful goals. You can love others for these same qualities because you may be coming to accept that the urgency of humanity's race toward recommitment to peace, love, and survival is ultimately a day-by-day process of change. And it is the wise man or woman who understands the nature of the race and the nature of the prize at the end.

Abundance

Abundance

PRESENT CIRCUMSTANCE
Creating all that you need at all levels for your life and in order to fulfill your vision for your planetary home.

You have drawn this card of Abundance as a means of shifting your inner and outer living into recognizable accomplishment, success, well-being, satisfaction, health, and mutual exchange with the human and natural systems that have partnered your advancement.

You have a vision for your life that has grown from your heart and from your spirit, a vision that tells you that you are a child of the Universe and are meant to grow in love, wisdom, and a cooperative attitude. You are meant to use your creativity, imagination, and abilities to the fullest extent in order to create a magnificent Earth home for you, those you love, and all the human beings and creatures in your planetary family.

ANGELIC MESSAGE
Abundance

You live in and with abundance when you accept the power of love to heal, transform, and create. Love is energy, and so when you invoke love for yourself, for others, and for the Earth, you bring universal energy into focus for specific manifestation of tangible materials and events.

Those who will be successful in creating and maintaining material advantage in the upcoming years are those to whom advantage over others means nothing. You will be coming into opportunities for specific financial advantages, and these will cause you to see how to reach out to accept these opportunities. Do you reach out only with your ego, which has its own needs to be met, or are you reaching to accept abundance so that you will have extra in order to return some to the natural sources from which your wealth has come?

When money, position, or other material advantages are offered, look beneath the surface of success, profit, or an important job title to see if abundance is truly present. Does the person you are doing business with, or do the circumstances from which you hope to make money, comply with the principles of universal abundance: to take only what is required in order to live reasonably upon the Earth, to use all human and natural resources for the benefit of all, and to proceed in all activities with a reverence for all life? If you accept this opportunity, through which physical resources of all kinds can flow, will you be free to express your gratitude and appreciation through a greater spiritual commitment to those who are still in need?

Abundance is a state of mind that leads to physical manifestation of physical resources. But, more important, abundance is a state of spirit that initially awakens the mind to its creative possibilities. You are being led toward abundant thinking, feeling, loving, and participating in life so that you will be in a position to encourage wholism in every form wherever you find it.

SPIRITUAL OPPORTUNITY

The guidance coming to you through this wild card is to accept the fluid beauty of spiritual conviction and allow it to manifest into multiple channels that will benefit you and many other living things. The flower image on this card symbolizes your present opportunity to realize diverse levels of achievement and improvement. The color green carries the energy of healing, which means you are being guided to heal old beliefs about your relationship with success and monetary advantage.

You are being asked to accept that in the future on your planet, those who successfully draw resources into manifestation will be those with a meaningful vision from which many avenues of success will flow. The Universe blesses the use of resources to support all living things equally. You will find increasing success coming to you so that you are in a better position to feed the same success back to others in order to encourage and heal them.

APPLICATION

Write out the ways in which you intend to use the abundance coming to you. List as many kinds of abundance, in addition to financial and monetary, as you can think of. Ask your children or the children of friends to share their lists of abundance. Write to your local newspaper editors and ask them to publish an article asking people to share with you the things that they consider important kinds of abundance. What becomes obvious to you and your family when you list the many kinds of meaningful abundance that you've discovered? Perhaps you'll find that abundance flows most directly from an attitude appreciating what you already have. When you are putting your present resources to good use, the Universe is more apt to offer you opportunities to do and to use more.

Divine

Guidance

Divine Guidance

PRESENT CIRCUMSTANCE
Opening your heart to love through direct experience with God and the angelic kingdom.

You have drawn this God-realization card because something significant and profoundly meaningful will further awaken you to the reality of the Divine in your life.

Expect that over the next several days you will be directly guided by the Universe. If you pay attention, you will have a significant realization of the heavenly kingdoms. You may perceive God's closeness in your life through an especially meaningful poem, reading, or vision. You may encounter the energy or spirit of a loved one who has died and wishes to share something with you. You may have an actual glimpse or perception of your angels, guides, or master teachers in a way that furthers your belief in the nonphysical world and in your own everlasting connection.

ANGELIC MESSAGE
Divine Guidance

Specific periods of spiritual opening occur at special moments throughout life. These moments are unique in that they draw you through the normal frustrations and contradictions toward acceptance of your loving relationship with the Universe.

You have entered such a time stream and are encouraged to open your inner eye as well as your outer vision, for you are being shown directly that you are loved eternally and that all is well at the spiritual level of your life. Pay attention to the subtleties of changes and events over the next few days. Allow yourself to be on alert to feeling a closer presence with God. No matter your past experiences or your immediate life path, you may be needing to understand at the heart level that you are on your spiritual path toward God-awareness.

We, your angelic teachers, ask you to accept that you are one energy with God and that your long-term best interests are always being considered. You may be feeling a need to truly accept that we and all of the heavenly kingdom are available to you. This is a time when any disbelief about yourself or the Universe can be dispelled. You may sometimes feel that God is too distant from your needs and concerns, or that Divinity is too impersonal or too "busy" to be involved with your simple emotional and physical aches and pains. The immense expanse that is God is aware of the simplest and smallest pain and is always present to you through every prayer and invocation.

Your intuition has guided you to this card because you may need reinforcement in your beliefs about yourself or others you love. Or you may feel lost or still be grieving the loss of someone you've loved who has moved on into spirit. And although you believe that the person goes on to greater joy and happiness, you feel left behind and lonely. Or you may feel rejected by others or by life, frustrated in your ability to understand your choices for the future, confused or ambivalent about which choices you should take. Or you may want only to share your joy and appreciation for the blessings in your life and to further deepen your ability to enter a sacred space in which God lives.

You are entering this sacred space of inner knowing in which the Universe is available to show you, intuit to you, open and make obvious for you, an aspect of its immortal presence that will help you in some true and lasting way.

SPIRITUAL OPPORTUNITY

The guidance to you through this extraordinary flower image is symbolically to release your fears, because all is held in eternal love, and there is nothing to be afraid of. The golden center of the flower is symbolically your natural ability to heal and expand in love. The illuminating white petals radiate out, speaking to you of the many lifetimes that you've lived and will continue to live.

You are guided to take a moment and reflect on the great expanse of opportunities that you hold because of your divine connection. You are capable of experiencing God's love as never before. You are guided to merely accept love into your life and to realize the compassion that moves with you through every life experience and challenge. You are asked to accept that you are blessed.

APPLICATION

Live the next several days as if they were a walking meditation. While you perform your normal chores and go to work or interact with others, look into the eyes of your family, friends, and colleagues. Silently bless their lives and their initiatives. Be observant and appreciative of the flowers, plants, trees, and animals that you see. Honor their presence. Speak to them, and tell them you appreciate their lives and their contributions to the Earth. Ask their help in healing the Earth. Intentionally give the planet only love, to the best of your ability, and keep from killing anything, even the smallest insect. Place your feet carefully on the Earth.

Take time to write down the feelings you experience during these next few days. Because you will be in a mildly altered state of consciousness, you will be able to perceive events and emotions with much greater clarity and perspective.

About the Photographer

Carol Duke regards flowers as "gestures from a divine source speaking directly to the soul." Trading her loom and weaving studio for a garden fork and the canvas of earth, Carol created "living tapestries" of hundreds of perennials, annuals, shrubs, and trees. Flower arranging evolved from the garden work as a kind of sketching.

As one client says, "Carol has at least in part a Japanese soul and has carried her skill in flower arranging to the highest art." Her stunning bouquets have graced weddings and galas for notable institutions, including the New York City Ballet.

"Photography became my way to record the ephemeral nature of flowers," Carol explains. "And the deeper I traveled into their folds and textures, the more I felt a consciousness there, alive and mirroring my own inner processes. That's what I hope to convey in my workshops and lectures."

Carol Duke lives and works in Williamsburg, Massachusetts.

About the Author

Meredith L. Young-Sowers is a nationally-known conference speaker, workshop leader, and author of books and audio tape programs in the New Thought and Spiritual Growth fields. Meredith is the author of *Spiritual Crisis: What's Really Behind Loss, Disease, and Life's Major Hurts*; the best-selling classic, *Agartha: A Journey to the Stars*; *Language of the Soul*; and the *Agartha Personal Life Balancing Program*.

Meredith is also co-publisher of Stillpoint Publishing in Walpole, New Hampshire, and co-founder and director of The Stillpoint Institute for Life Healing. As the featured subject of numerous magazine articles as well as guest speaker on many national radio talk shows, she focuses on developing tools of the spirit for self-empowerment and personal transformation.

She resides with her husband and family in Walpole, New Hampshire.

Other Books and Resources

Item #010, $11.95
ISBN 0-913299-01-4

Agartha: A Journey to the Stars

Discover your own power to become attuned to the non-physical world. A best-selling classic, *Agartha* is a guide to essential spiritual truths. Here Meredith Lady Young relates the story of her journey into a world few of us know how to enter. As you read this fascinating book, you can find empowerment and share in the wisdom of her non-physical teacher, Mentor.

Item #036 $12.50
ISBN 0-913299-52-9

Language of the Soul: Applying Universal Principles for Self-Empowerment

The exercises in this self-paced workbook will guide you toward new levels of perception and the truth about the spiritual ground rules that frame your life experiences. The chapter on creating your "personal power mandala" is alone well worth the price, for here Meredith teaches you how to identify "the face you show to the world," the issues and spiritual qualities you must understand to achieve satisfaction, happiness and growth, and the "vehicles through which you feel you can fulfill your life purpose."

by Meredith L. Young-Sowers

Item #125, $13.95
ISBN 0-913299-89-8

Spiritual Crisis: What's Really Behind Loss, Disease, and Life's Major Hurts

Spiritual crisis gives us an opportunity "to pay close attention to our feelings, insights, beliefs, and thoughts. It can be a new beginning, awakening us to fresh insights, energy, and creativity." With clear guidelines and step-by-step techniques, Meredith helps us understand the patterns behind our losses and failures, as well as our life lessons and life themes, so that we can move forward into a life of renewed meaning and depth.

Item #002, seven tapes: $59.95
        ISBN 0-913299-59-6
**Individual tapes available
at $9.95 each:**
Earth Connection   Item #300
Emotional/Sexual Balance   #301
Personal Power   #302
Love   #303
Communication   #304
Intuition   #305
Spiritual Questing   #306

Agartha Personal Life-Balancing Program

The sounds on these tape recordings are excellent for reducing stress and improving the flow of energy throughout your body.

These seven harmonic tapes combine sounds that were developed to alter the energy currents within a specific energy center (chakra) of the body. This thirty-five day program has been used effectively by thousands.

The Stillpoint Institute
for Life Healing

If you are seeking to strengthen the spiritual work you've already begun and are interested in meaningful group participation or spiritual community, then The Stillpoint Institute for Life Healing has much to offer you.

The Institute for Life Healing is an important extension of our commitment both to grow spiritually and to establish community with others who share the same desires. Through the process of personal discovery and group support, we are better able to stay balanced and to live our spirituality with others even when they have a different philosophy and play by different "rules."

Consider joining with others around the planet to take that next crucial spiritual step. Link up with others who are also moving through change and want to share their stories and give and receive love. Become a member of The Stillpoint Institute and help create these essential forums for spiritual growth and support.

When you become a member of The Stillpoint Institute for Life Healing, you will receive:

- **Ten issues of THE STILLPOINT FORUM,** which feature four focused spiritual lessons and divinely-inspired insights; (one for each week of the month), a special section with specific information and study materials useful for monthly study groups or Life Healing Circles; shared insights by members; thoughtful guest essays; a calendar of events.
- **An audio tape and guide booklet** by Meredith Young-Sowers to help you and your friends facilitate and engage in group process by creating **LIFE HEALING CIRCLES.**
- **Many other blessings and benefits.**

TO BECOME A MEMBER OR TO ASK FOR
FURTHER INFORMATION ABOUT THE
STILLPOINT INSTITUTE FOR LIFE HEALING,
CALL STILLPOINT AT
800-847-4014
